I0163947

Touring 1938 Europe Unawares

Memoir of SS Normandie Sailing to Pre WWII Europe Including Nazi Germany

Helen and a French Sailor On the SS Normandie

Kathleen A. Reed

Copyright © 2011 by 1938 Publishing Company

All rights reserved. No part of this book may be reproduced or transmitted in any form or by any means, graphic, electronic or mechanical, including photocopying, recording, taping or by any information storage or retrieval system, without permission in writing from the publisher.

ISBN 978-0-9838196-0-8

Manufactured in the United States of America

Email the author: 1938diary@earthlink.net

Web Site:
www.touring1938europeunawares.com

Preface

This is a true story, taken from the pages of Helen McPhail's leather bound trip diaries. The narrative includes sailing aboard the SS Normandie and the RMS Queen Mary, and traveling by rail through nine European countries. Every evening of her two month journey, Helen meticulously logged the adventures of the day into her journals. She passed down these diaries to me along with photos, ephemera and the carbon copy of a travelogue letter she wrote to a friend in 1939. Because the letter was so rich with extra details, I carefully blended it with the text from the diaries. This unique combination of experiences simply must be shared!

Helen was a single lady of thirty years, with a Masters Degree in mathematics. She worked for the US Government Department of Agriculture, in Washington D.C. The trip was prepaid so she traveled with coupons, tickets, and vouchers, for the hotels, trains and tours, plus a tight budget for souvenirs. Upon arrival at each train station, she was to be met by a representative of her hotel. That did not always happen. She traveled with a friend but at midpoint of the trip, they went in separate directions, as planned. Upon her arrival at Nuremberg, the twists and turns commenced.

The title "Touring 1938 Europe Unawares" embodies the mindset of Americans, Europeans - and for that matter, world leaders - when it came to the aftermath of Hitler's annexation of Austria (5 months before her trip.) The prevailing sentiment was that another war was to be avoided at almost any cost. It was assumed (or leaders wanted to believe) that Hitler would be satisfied with his acquisitions of Austria and the Sudetenland portion of Czecho-slovakia. 1938 was a significant year in the prelude to World War II. If people knew then, what we know now, how many tourists would have included Austria or Germany in their autumn of 1938 itinerary?

Traveling throughout foreign countries can catch any of us "unawares" with respect to culture, traditions, and the weather. However if you add the possibility of war breaking out, life can become very unpredictable. Helen observed evidence of military occupation but tourism seemed to proceed as a matter of course. She was not threatened with physical harm but did encounter several disturbing experiences during her journey.

Helen embraced the philosophy that every time something unexpected happened, new and exciting experiences would follow. Possessing an outgoing nature, she was motivated to learn about people she encountered, regardless of their native language. She communicated fairly well due to her college courses in German and French, resorting when necessary to using sketches and sign language.

Be sure to read the epilogue which includes copies of letters from soldiers she met in Europe. Bon Voyage!

Editor's Note: I believe that when Helen writes about the Conservatory on the SS Normandie, she is referring to what was called the Winter Garden.

You will see photos of, and read about encounters with, several Austrian or German soldiers. It is never my intent to present these men in a positive or negative light, but just to relay what was in the diary and her scrapbook. Helen was as unaware as most people, when it came to the inhumanities that were already taking place. Even most German citizens were kept in the dark by control of the media.

I have attempted to research every detail of this trip, with respect to the accuracy of dates, names, places, spelling, and grammar. At times it was difficult to read her handwriting. Although I did my best, it is possible that some details are not 100% accurate.

The photos were taken from her scrapbook. I made them as crisp as possible. Even though they are not altogether perfect, they are important to the story.

Acknowledgements

This book would not have been possible without the support of my family and friends, who encouraged me to fulfill my aunt's wishes to share her unique pre-WWII experiences with the reading public.

I am extremely grateful to my Aunt Helen who kept track of the details of her journey and preserved the photos for so many years. I consider Helen the real author of this book.

I am also sincerely thankful to Sylvia Diedrich, who enthusiastically took on the task of expertly translating a letter that the Austrian soldier, Max, wrote to my aunt, after the end of WWII.

ACKNOWLEDGMENTS

[illegible]

[illegible]

[illegible]

Table of Contents

1

Washington D.C. to New York, And Sailing the SS Normandie

Date: August 2, 1938
Place: Washington DC to New York City
Weather: Everything was perfect

What an exciting day, from beginning to end! After a mad scramble, Margy and I arrived at the train station toting our beautifully labeled luggage! We had asked the taxi driver to stop at places all over Washington D.C., so we could pick up some last minute things. I was so crazy happy when we arrived at the train station that I almost forgot to pay the cab driver - even with the money clutched in my hand!

Our friends Elsie, Edwina and Stella, were at the station when we arrived. They gave us a big send-off which included a stunning bouquet of roses, icy cold fruit and many good wishes. The train ride seemed quite short because Margy and I talked continually. Upon leaving the train, we boarded a gorgeous private bus that took us to the Victoria Hotel. During the ride, we caught our first glimpse of the SS Normandie ship. So stunning was the sight of this enormous ocean liner, that for once we were speechless!

After settling into our room, we took a taxicab to 52nd Street, in New York City. We strolled past the little foreign dives and dined at the Chalet Suisse, which was a delightful place. I ordered slowly smoked Westphelian ham, after the waiter said it was imported from Germany. Before too long, we will be in Germany, enjoying the unique food and wine.

After dinner, we proceeded to The Radio City Music Hall, where the magnificent decor far exceeded my expectations. The opulent splendor of the place left us breathless! On my next visit to New York, I would love to see a musical or stage show, but tonight we viewed the movie, "Algiers," which starred Charles Boyer and Hedy Lamarr. It is difficult to wind down to anything as plebian as sleep, after such an exciting day.

Date: August 3, 1938
Place: New York and Aboard the SS Normandie
Weather: HOT! No doubt!

Today has been a dream and more. We departed our hotel for the Normandie at 9:30 a.m. There it was, waiting for passengers and appearing even larger than it had yesterday. After passing through ticket and passport examination, Margy and I walked up the long gangplank, passing by rows of red-capped bellhops who were standing at attention, until we were finally on board!

The ship was so vast that one moment we wandered around happily, and the next we were hopelessly lost. We just giggled, twirled around, and darted off in another direction.

The temperature in New York today, was heading for 96 degrees, and we nearly perished! We were not dressed for such hot weather because our destination is Europe, where it will be cooler.

Friends and relatives, who came to see us off, were allowed to visit us on the ship. We had been dashing around so much that they had a hard time finding us! It was such fun chatting with them while taking in the wonders of our surroundings.

A few passengers were whispering that movie actress Simone Simon was on board, as well as Kitty Carlisle and financier Bernard Baruch.

Helen on deck, wearing her gardenia corsage

Before too long, it was necessary for our guests to leave the ship. The S.S. Normandie dramatically pulled away with all the flurry of a moving-picture-type departure! Gigantic whistles were blowing and screeching, accompanied by wild hand-wavings between ship and shore. We about fainted from the heat, while standing at the ship railing in the sunshine.

Chapter 1: Sailing the SS Normandie

SS Normandie departure with passengers at the rail

The SS Normandie as it sailed away

Margy and I chose to sail tourist class on this ship, which is well known for being predominately a luxury liner. Just imagine our happiness when we found ourselves in the "interchangeable quarters!" The cabins in our section of the ship are used for First Class on some trips and for Tourist on others.

Our cabin is gorgeous! We have two grand beds - with a longhaired white rug between them - and two washbasins if you please! There is a dressing table, two bureaus, and little twin bedside tables. It really is magnificent! We have separate mirror-lined wardrobes, and there is a nook just for our suitcases. In addition to a writing desk with chair, there is a lovely comfy chair. We were tickled by the private bathroom with a washbasin, toilet, and the cutest shower I have seen. It comes out from the sides and caresses you, making it difficult to tear yourself away. There is an extra washbasin enclosed in a door so that if one person is in the bathroom the other can use that basin.

Our room is softly fragranced with the most colorful flowers! Mother and Dad sent a vase of tall gladioli spikes, which I will have transported to our dining room table. There are pink roses and white asters from Uncle Paul. I am wearing the prettiest gardenia corsage, which will be stored in our refrigerator, overnight. Telegrams arrived by the dozens! We are just crazy with excitement!

Bon Voyage Telegrams sent to the SS Normandie

The afternoon on the Normandie just flew by. We have been assigned dining room seating at a table for four near a porthole. Dinner is served (for the second sitting) at 8:30 p.m. Our dining companions turned out to be a couple of well-seasoned male travelers, who tell us that they are doctors from New York City. Hy and Bernie often adopt a blasé attitude, but then again, they can act crazy and be lots of fun! After tonight's feast, the four of us strolled the deck and gazed at the reflection of the moon on the ocean. It is early to bed (12:30 a.m.) for a big day tomorrow.

Date: August 4, 1938
Place: On Board the Normandie
Weather: A little cooler, but still hot!

When the alarm went off at 8 a.m. this morning, it felt like it should be the middle of the night. Noticing that the clocks had advanced an entire half-hour overnight, I made a mad scramble for breakfast.

The clocks are advanced to compensate for the time changes, as we make our way to Europe. Right after breakfast, I went with our two doctors on a tour of the ship. Hy presented me with a rose from the dining room, and they were both acting crazy, as usual. Bernie now tells me that he is a veterinarian, but I cannot believe a thing they say; they are so silly.

The first-class area certainly is spacious and grand and the dining room is lovely beyond description. The walls and chandeliers sparkle with brilliant glass. I am told that this room holds well over 600 diners, and that the chandelier glass was made by Lalique.

The conservatory is an amazing place – with wild and cultivated flowers, fountains, and real birds. I certainly never expected to hear birds chirping on a ship! The walls are adorned with murals which are painted on canvas, glass, and wood. I could just sit there forever and ever!

I tiptoed into the darling chapel where they hold church services on Sunday. All of the woodcarvings in this chapel were created by blind people – such intricate and beautiful work!

In the afternoon, we (by very special permission) were allowed to see the engines! Hy and Bernie helped me coax the purser, because women are not supposed to go into the engine room. The only stipulation was that I wear slacks or shorts. Margy wanted to take a nap, so I borrowed a pair of her shorts, which turned out to be very short on me!

The expanse of leg that I displayed caused more attention than I would have wished.

Well, back to the tour! The engine rooms are mammoth and appear as clean as any salon. It surely was hot down there, but we were so happy that we had the opportunity to see it all! After locating Margy, we went on deck to watch the fellows shoot at clay pigeons.

It seems that we do nothing more than eat and get ready to eat. For such a large ship as the Normandie, social life is not at all organized. There are no planned activities to help you become acquainted with the other passengers. You have to make your own friends and plan your own entertainment. The only people that you meet on a regular basis are those who sit at your dining table and next to your assigned deck chair.

Helen relaxing in a deck chair, on the SS Normandie

Our deck chairs overlook the swimming pool, so we have a grand view of everything. The deck steward was most gracious in assigning them to us, but we do not have the opportunity to spend as much time in them as we would like.

There are plenty of things to do, all day long, including attending concerts, which we especially love. One can swim in the pool, go to movies, dance, and participate in all sorts of deck sports.

Hy, Margy and Bernie, kidding around on deck

Date: August 5, 1938
Place: On Board the Normandie
Weather: Perfect - much cooler in morning

We can dine anywhere we choose in the morning. At breakfast we chatted with a lovely couple. The husband was such an Adonis of a man! However, he still cannot compete with the handsome Purser's assistant, whose dreamy deep blue eyes have me completely subjected.

Swimming pool on the SS Normandie, Helen center

This was such a lazy morning, that it was difficult to summon ambition to do anything more than swim in the outdoor pool! The temperature was swell as long as you stayed in the water. Hy and Bernie reacted like two big sissies, when I invited them to join me for a swim. They said they preferred to sit and watch me swim. After lunch, we went on deck and fooled around, laughing and finding out more about each other. We played questions and answers.

At 4:30, the four of us went to the movies to see Joan Blondell and Melvyn Douglas in the hilarious film, "There's Always a Woman." Then it was time to dress for dinner - which takes us at least an hour. After dining, we moved up on deck for some conversation and dancing. I had one dance with Hy, and then I became extremely distressed when Bernie could not dance! He said that he had been sick. Margy and Hy were out gallivanting somewhere, so I was stuck sitting with Bernie. It will not be that way tomorrow night, because I so love to dance! I will try to subtly drift away from Bernie, and seek out a dance partner.

PS: The theater is like a real little playhouse, seating 380 people! The walls are delicately patterned with silver leaf. The stage curtain looks like velvet, except that it shimmers.

Date: August 6, 1938
Place: On Board the Normandie
Weather: Foggy - warmer

Before the sun came up this morning, we awoke suddenly when the ship seemed to lurch to a stop! Frightened to death, we rushed out into the hallway and heard a man say that ships naturally slow down for foggy conditions. It was difficult to calm down, so we slept in, and enjoyed breakfast in bed. We had stayed up until 2:00 a.m. this morning. What hours one keeps on a ship! To work up an appetite, we went swimming before lunch. Our attempt to play a little shuffleboard, ended in frustration and waves of laughter. I could not even make the markers (or whatever you call them) go all the way! We will leave that sport to someone else.

Oh, by the way, the Purser is getting so he recognizes me. This afternoon he smiled and nicely said "Good Morning!" However, it is his assistant, a handsome looking brute, who causes my heart to flutter.

"Test Pilot" was the afternoon movie today. Tonight we attended a party and OH! What a party! The chefs prepared an extra-special dinner with an exquisitely decorated cake. This delightful meal was followed by entertainment and dancing in the salon. It was a crazy swell time and everyone was rip-roaring. Hy and Bernie are becoming irrepressible. We were with them most of the evening, although we danced with others as well.

Date: August 7, 1938
Place: On Board the Normandie
Weather: Coolish

After arising at 8 a.m., I dashed off a letter before breakfast. I suspect that many passengers were resting up from the big party last evening, as there were very few people eating breakfast. Since it was quite early, I settled down amongst the orchids in the tranquil conservatory, and wrote my letters to the tune of warbling birds.

I strolled into first class to find the chapel, and attended a church service at 11:00 a.m. The sermon was lovely, however the minister seemed a bit too informal for such a breathtaking setting. After rooting Margy out of bed, we spent the remainder of the day lounging on the deck, attending movies, and packing. We engaged in a frenzy of picture taking, as we will be leaving the SS Normandie before too long.

Because tonight is our last night on the ship, we were told to have our suitcases packed and ready to be removed from the cabin by 6 p.m. All we could keep to ourselves was one small bag. I asked the Purser (he actually called me by name) and his bee-oo-ti-ful assistant to sign their autographs on this diary. My heart still has not returned to normal.

We had another grand dinner tonight - our last dinner on the Normandie. It is early to bed tonight and up early in the morning, for the sunrise and debarkation at Southampton, England. Whoopee!

2

England and Scotland

Date: August 8, 1938
Place: National Hotel, London, England
Weather: Grand!

It will be difficult to squeeze all the details of this day into the diary. Nearly everyone was roused out of bed at some unearthly hour this morning but our kind steward let us sleep until 6:00 a.m.

The Normandie docked at Southampton so early that we did not get out on deck in time to see the approaching shoreline. The landing was perfect, with grand sunlight and beautiful clouds! This was not the customary weather, according to one Englishman. After a hurried dressing and last-minute packing, we dashed off to our final breakfast on the Normandie. Our fellow passengers looked so different in their landing clothes. The stewards were all on deck to wish us a lovely trip. We gave them their tips, took some last minute pictures, and said our fond good-byes.

The RMS Queen Mary actually docks at this location, however the SS Normandie, being a French Ship, places departing passengers on a tender that takes them to shore.

After a brief wait, we embarked on the tender (Grove Field) for the two-hour trip to Southampton. Since there was time to spare, we were given a sightseeing tour near the Isle of Wight and into the harbor. We passed by the castle where Queen Victoria formerly lived. Her 90-year-old sister, Louise, resides there now and is honorary governor of the island.

After having our passports carefully examined, we were happily reunited with our bags. Everyone was so pleasant and patient with us. I brought along eight packs of cigarettes to use as a little thank-you to folks like these, who were so helpful. A travel agent met us at Southampton, and directed us to the boat train. We sat in the cutest little compartment amongst other passengers from the Normandie, including Hy and Bernie. By this time we were all dopey and hungry, but the views of the countryside kept us conscious. As the train whizzed along we were captivated by the thatched roofs and neat gardens. A representative of our tour company met us upon arrival in London. After bidding farewell to Hy and Bernie, accompanied by lots of hugs, we followed our tour operator to a bus, which transported us to the Hotel National.

Our hotel is a native hotel, unlike those that were built specifically for tourists. It is so very native that we had to adjust quickly to the British customs and language differences. The actions of the room maids are one of the most curious sights we have seen yet. They have a manner of bobbing up and down quite humorously, making it difficult for one to keep from giggling! The maids all wear black stockings, and don white hair caps and aprons like those we made while taking sewing class in school. The old elevators creep up and down so slowly that they are furnished with places for people to sit!

Margy and I have separate rooms. My room is most peculiar, with red window shades and atrocious wallpaper. (I shall have nightmares!) There is just enough floor space to turn around. We had lunch at an ABC Store then explored downtown London. We settled on a J. Lyons & Co. teashop for dinner. This was one of several J. Lyons teashops in London, but it still has a quaint atmosphere. We conversed with many people, just to experience and absorb the English way of speaking. After driving folks near us crazy with a million questions about busses and exchanging money, we finally returned to our hotel.

Date: August 9, 1938
Place: London (and vicinity)
Weather: Typical – rained off and on all day

We awakened early and enjoyed a hotel breakfast of bacon and eggs (after refusing porridge.) Elsie's advice about taking our umbrellas, whether or not it looked like rain, was most helpful. Out of the beautiful sunny skies, intermittent showers descended throughout the day. Before leaving for the tourist office, we needed to arrange for theater tickets. We looked all over for the deskman, and found him outside, scrubbing the steps. I guess it was too early for him to don his hotel uniform. He seemed a bit huffy, but I think his dignity was a little bruised to have been caught doing such a menial task. We are struggling to sense the proper way to conduct ourselves here in England.

A taxicab took us to the tourist office for our bus ride to Oxford, Warwick, and Stratford. The grand courier on the bus seemed overwhelmed by our numerous questions. He was a very good-natured soul and offered some valuable advice about our upcoming excursions. After a long drive through interesting parts of London, we stopped first at Magdalen College. The Duke of Windsor attended this school. While we were in the chapel, I actually sat down in the Duke's personal seat – but I still felt the same afterwards!

As we proceeded to Oxford, the tour guide pointed out places that dated back as far as the fourteenth century! He confided that in current times, young men seldom attend Oxford for more than one year. They just want to have it on their record that they attended Oxford!

Amidst showers of raindrops, we proceeded to the medieval Warwick Castle, perched high on a bluff, overlooking the bend of the River Avon. We then hurried on to Stratford where Shakespeare and Ann

Hathaway lived. Both places were surrounded by the loveliest gardens. Even the rain could not hide their beauty. Tomorrow is another big day, so off to bed.

Date: August 10, 1938
Place: London and Vicinity
Weather: Raining!

Authentic London weather presided, as we splashed around all day in the rain. This morning we took a tour of the city and viewed the exteriors of many important buildings. Because of the weather, we regrettably missed the ceremony of the changing of the guard. Thank goodness, the rain could not keep us from seeing the inside of St Paul's Cathedral. It appeared so huge that I wondered how the congregations could hear the services. The beautiful stained glass windows were rivaled only by the delicate oak woodcarvings.

An inside visit to the Tower of London, where Royal Jewels worth $25,000,000 are displayed, dazzled our eyes. I never dreamed there were so many jeweled crowns, tiaras, scepters, and swords in the world! We viewed the other six towers, the moat and surrounding grounds. Our guide pointed out the spot where persons of royalty were executed on the gallows. As one gazes about the Tower of London grounds, you see large black birds that are called ravens. We were informed that ravens have always lived here. In fact as legend has it, if the ravens ever leave, the monarchy and the tower itself will fall.

After lunch at Lyons, we joined a tour to Windsor, Eton, plus the Hampton Court Palace. The rain was relentless. It is hard to conceive of the antiquity of things over here. The mammoth Windsor Castle is magnificent, and it fully lives up to any storybook description of a palace built for a king. Our last stop was Hampton Court Palace, which was constructed in 1515. The park is 750 acres in size, and contains gardens, ponds, and many varieties of birds. It was a nice surprise to see the resident herd of deer strolling the grounds. Our guide said that they are quite tame.

This evening Margy and I hopped a bus to Madame Tussauds Wax Works. The full size wax figures appear so lifelike that you expect them to move. It is easy to feel embarrassed when a man of wax seems to be staring at you intently. One of the figures actually has a breathing contraption. The chamber of horrors is horrible indeed, and I certainly preferred the other displays. We are becoming quite the experts on the London busses now and can exit without having to be told "when." I think we will try the subway, next.

Date: August 11, 1938
Place: London, England
Weather: Grand! Chilly in a.m., warm in p.m.

Today was the busiest day yet! We explored on our own and returned home this evening, thoroughly tired. Our first stop was The British Museum, with its ancient Egyptian sculptures, mummies, and the Rosetta Stone. As time was fleeting by, we hurried to see the National Art Gallery at Trafalgar Square.

There we viewed the originals of many well-known paintings by artists such as Gainsborough, Titian and Van Dyke.

The next stop was Westminster Abbey, where we were very fortunate! One of the ministerial assistants there took an interest in us and he escorted us on a thorough tour of the Abbey! It was a perfect way to see the place and we learned so much more than we would have on our own. I loved the chapel of King Henry VII. The morning light was streaming through the breathtaking stained glass windows. The great organ with its four keyboards and hundreds of stops amazed us. Londoners seem to recognize that we are Americans, and are very kind in directing us. I cannot tell you how grateful we are!

We had lunch at the famous Cheshire Cheese restaurant, feasting on roast beef, Cheshire cheese and cider. Well, I thought I would keep my senses by choosing the cider instead of ale. Alas, one sip revealed that my drink was a very hard cider, indeed.

Strolling along the Thames embankment, we stopped to enjoy the Royal Sussex band in concert. A long ride out to Kensington Gardens was next on the list, where we saw hundreds of children playing about and feeding the birds. The sweet little tots frolicked beneath a delightful Statue of Peter Pan! A visitor is welcome to sit anywhere they choose, but they must pay 2D for a seat.

We hurried back to town, stopping for a small tea, before going to the Victoria Palace Theater to see a stage play featuring Lupino Lane and George Graves in "Me and My Girl." Lupino Lane is the comedian who popularized the song "The Lambeth Walk."

The difference between the English and American entertainment style certainly manifested itself in this musical comedy. The English sense of humor is distinctly along the slapstick line. They are just about where we in America were, ten years ago.

Their humor was a bit raw at times, however quite amusing. The audience just howled! They actually fell out of their seats! At the end of the performance, they all stood up to sing. We sang "*America*" right along with them but they thought we were singing "*God Save the King*." (Same melody)

Date: August 12, 1938
Place: London
Weather: Usual London weather; cold and raining

Just to be different, I started out the morning with a big dish of English porridge, served by the prettiest waitress. She was like a little English rose, in spite of the awful costume she has to wear. We were very excited about exploring the Caledonian Market, also known as the rag market. They say it is one of THE sights of London! Open only on Tuesdays and Fridays, it draws all sorts and all classes of people. Word was flying around that Edward Everett Horton and Sylvia Sidney were spotted there this morning.

The merchants put up stalls, and then sell all sorts of things - mostly second hand. We were very tempted by the many offerings of antiques, silverware, and jewelry. It was so much fun examining the items, and trying to decide if they were worth purchasing. A shopper never considers paying the price that the merchants ask; he bargains with them until the amount is reduced 40% to 50%. I bought a set of little silver spoons with Shakespearian characters molded on the handles, a turquoise matrix ring, and a curious little silver filigree pin. I hope that they were bargains but a good polishing and a jeweler's verdict will tell.

Soon after we finished lunch, the storm clouds gathered, so we hurried to a bus and rode downtown to Selfridges. This is London's largest department store, where Margy did some purchasing and I did some looking. One could spend an entire day in this enormous store. The variety of things to select from is beyond compare. We had planned to purchase something to wear, but the clothes were so hopelessly old fashioned and drab, we decided to wait until we are in Paris. How can Londoners be so particular about their gardens and parks, yet dress so ordinary looking as a people? This is especially noticeable in the general dowdy appearance of the women. As one Frenchman put it – they are so solid! That is a perfect description. The British men are good looking, but they run around with such plainly dressed females! Oh well! The Englishmen seem to like them that way, and that is what matters.

A short visit to a Woolworth's 3D & 6D store revealed that it is very similar to our American Woolworth's 5 & 10¢ Stores. Since it was raining hard, we went to a Newsreel Theater to pass the time before dinner. I guess we were tired, because I slept through the first part of the show and Margy dozed through the remainder.

By now, we were ready for a special dinner at the popular Simpsons in the Strand. Their meat carver man wheels his little cart of delicious beef right up to your chair and asks you what part you wish to have sliced. There is an open fire under the platter that keeps food hot, and cooks some pieces more than others. Everyone in the restaurant - both the waiters and diners - seemed to be staring at us. We decided that they were looking at our funny American hats. After dinner, listening again to the Royal Sussex Regiment Band in the Victoria Embankment Gardens was the perfect way to finish the evening.

Date: August 13, 1938
Place: Keswick, England
Weather: Cold – believe it or not - but so nice

Tonight I am sitting in bed covered with lots of blankets and a cozy eiderdown comforter. We adore our room here at the Royal Oak Hotel. We left London at Noon for Keswick. It was a long, dirty train ride but the countryside held our attention. What an experience, eating on the train! A conductor strutted down the aisle shouting, "First sitting," or "Second sitting," and then handed us a little card, according to our choice. We picked the second sitting. When he called out a sitting, the people dashed madly behind him into the dining car. Everyone ate the same thing, all at once, and downed it as rapidly as possible. It seemed like a race to see who could eat the quickest.

As the train gradually approached the mountains, the countryside grew lovelier. We stopped right in the midst of all this beauty, at Keswick. It is a little bit of heaven – although a rather chilly heaven. After dinner, I took a walk down to Derwentwater Lake, which is dotted with islands. With the majestic mountains mirrored in the placid water, the view could inspire one to poetry! If Switzerland is as lovely as Keswick, I shall be most happy.

Date: August 14, 1938
Place: Keswick England
Weather: Perfect, but a little chilly

It is amazing the way these English gals run around in thin, short sleeved dresses, while we freeze in our suits! This has been a perfect day, weather and all. After rising early this morning, I took the 8:00 bus to Lodore Falls. The Falls were not as prolific as expected, (considering the recent rainfall) but the frothy water did tumble and splash over the large boulders. The surroundings were most beautiful. I wandered along the bank, climbing over smaller boulders that were draped in rich green moss. I almost fell once, and nearly lost my shoe, another time. That was a grand little exploration trip.

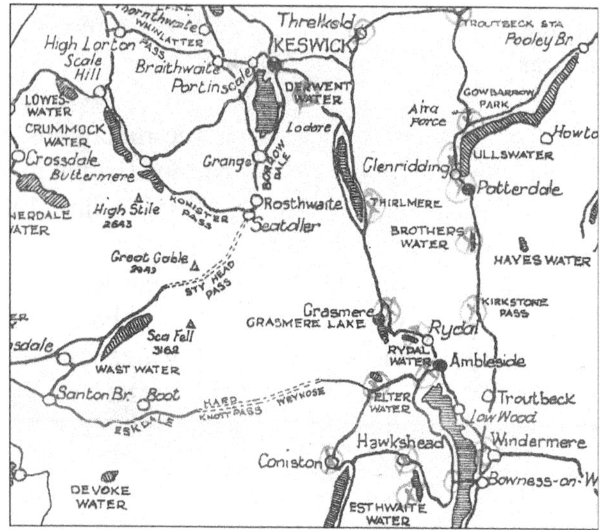

Map of the English Lakes Tour

I returned to Keswick in time to take a walk down to the lake with Margy, before embarking on our tour of the 11 lakes. We certainly enjoyed that trip. We met a dark and good-looking fellow from the Malay States, who was on an eight-month holiday trip of England. He seemed quite taken with Margy and invited us to tea.

The mountains and lakes were lovelier than anything I have seen. Stone fences ambled all over the sides of the mountains. We went through several wicket gates and I saw a good old-fashioned stile. We loved the purple hazes of heather growing on hillsides, but I am waiting to pick some heather in Scotland, where my Grandfather McPhail was born.

Chapter 2: England and Scotland

Date: August 15, 1938
Place: Keswick to Glasgow
Weather: Fair but definitely chilly, except in sun

Even though we arranged for morning transportation to the train station, no one showed up at our hotel! In desperation, I begged for help from a complete stranger. He was very gracious and accommodating, so we arrived at the station just in time! The journey to Glasgow (Scotland's largest city) was nice, albeit a long one. We obtained a non-smoking carriage, and therein met the cutest little Scottish boy named Stuart MacDonald. He was adorable and we kept asking him questions just to hear his accent. Margy and I had struggled greatly to understand the English accent and pronunciation, but the minute we struck Scotland and heard the first touch of brogue, my ancestors came to my assistance and I just loved it. We could listen to the Scottish talk all day.

The train arrived in Glasgow at 2:30 but no one met us! There must have been a mix-up, for the hotel had no record of our reservation! We secured a nice room at the North British Hotel, and then sallied forth to view *No. 10 Nelson*, where my Grandfather McPhail was born. We arrived there on a bus and were greatly chagrinned to find an elevated railway track where No. 10 used to be. The closest thing to it was a hole in the wall marked "*Gentlemen.*"

Next was a visit to the Empire Exhibition, where we rode around the grounds on a miniature railway train that had a diesel engine. We also took a daring elevator ride to the top of the 300-foot high

modernistic tower. A shallow little pond with many fountains displayed beautiful colors when lit up at night. I had a dreadful time pulling myself away from the Scottish souvenirs, but limited my purchases to some cards for Dad.
PS: The square outside our window is decorated with colored lights and it looks just like Christmas time.

Date: August 16, 1938
Place: On the way to - and in Edinburgh
Weather: Cold and rainy

After an early breakfast, we arranged to have our bags checked thru to Edinburgh so we could enjoy the Trossachs tour free of luggage. It started to rain just about the time we left the hotel in Glasgow and it continued more or less all day. It was so cold! In ordinary weather, this Highland trip would have been glorious. We took a train to Ballock Pier, on the south end of Loch Lomond. Our boat drifted past many small green islands, of which there are dozens, depending on the water level. In spite of the gray skies, the countryside was most colorful with the green grass and purple heather. We had lunch at the Trossachs Hotel, then caught the train to Edinburgh.

Date: August 17, 1938
Place: Edinburgh, Scotland
Weather: Rather chilly, very windy, but NO RAIN!

It certainly is cold up in this part of the country and I would give a ransom for a hot water bottle at my feet right now. We started the day with shopping, then headed for Edinburgh Castle. The castle, built on an extinct volcano, dominates the area. Even if you are not facing it, you can just feel it towering over you. Perched high above the city, it looks just like the castles you read about in fairy tales. One can see for miles from the castle courtyard. We followed a guide through the castle and learned that the moat was never filled with water, because the castle was too high! The drawbridge, instead of drawing up, drops down.

All of this uniqueness was the result of an error in engineering. We saw the seven gates, and heard a loud boom from the cannon that goes off every day at 1:00 pm.

After tea, we spent the rest of the day shopping in Edinburgh, where I purchased many plaid things.

Helen, in earlier times, kidding around with her Uncle Paul

ASSOCIATED BRITISH
AND IRISH RAILWAYS
(INCORPORATED)
GREAT WESTERN · LONDON & NORTH EASTERN
LONDON MIDLAND & SCOTTISH · SOUTHERN RAILWAYS
and
GREAT SOUTHERN RAILWAYS OF IRELAND
9 ROCKEFELLER PLAZA - NEW YORK CITY
333 NORTH MICHIGAN AVENUE
CHICAGO
412 WEST SIXTH STREET
LOS ANGELES
TRAVEL BUREAU R. M. S. "QUEEN MARY"

Booklet of railway tickets (color is light blue)

3

Holland and Belgium

Date: August 18, 1938
Place: Overnight crossing to The Hague
Weather: Chilly but fair

Thank goodness, it was not necessary for us to change trains during our 11-hour ride to Chadwick, although we did grow weary of sitting. After boarding the boat to The Hague, we realized that it was fun riding on a steamer ship again. The throbbing of the engines is a pleasant sensation.

The staterooms are tiny and the boat is rather crowded. We purchased some Dutch money, and now have the opportunity to adapt to a new currency.

Here's for a smooth overnight crossing!

Date: August 19, 1938
Place: Holland – all over
Weather: Grand - but dreadfully windy

We were up at 5 a.m., and ready to land shortly before 6 a.m. They say it was a rough crossing but I will have to confess to remembering little about it except being nicely rocked to sleep. Upon landing, we were graciously greeted by a tour representative.

The Dutch customs officials did not open even one of our bags. We found the bus that was going to The Hague. The driver let us off in front of our hotel, *The Terminus*, which is across from the railway station. It is a lovely hotel – so spacious, open, and very modern. Our neat and clean bedroom is immense! A little pincushion on the dresser provides us with sewing needles, which contain black and white thread. After breakfast, we joined several others for a Grand Motor Tour of Holland, and it was indeed grand! Holland's tulip bulbs can now be exported, so I purchased a couple of boxes. The Dutch houses are so quaint, with the doors and windows being bright and shiny. We saw for the first time, the little mirrors (on the sides of buildings) called "*busy bodies*" that enable the housewives to keep track of everything that is going on up and down the street.

One cannot visit this area without seeing the cheese market! It certainly is an interesting spectacle, with the colorful native costumes, crowds of people, and piles of fragrant cheese. We passed by the dikes holding back the Zuiderzee – a shallow bay of the North Sea. Recently they have succeeded in cutting the Zuiderzee off from the ocean completely. A boat took us to the Isle of Markem, where the people are even more distinct in their costumes and customs. One gets the feeling though, that these activities are chiefly for the benefit of the tourists.

The trip homeward took us through Amsterdam, with its 37 canals and the Jewish Ghetto. Automobiles are uncommon in Holland. While waiting for a stop light to change, it was strange to see only a large group of bicycles. The Dutch staff at our hotel kept things so clean and neat. If we left something out of place in our room, when we returned it would be straightened up. In Amsterdam, we visited a diamond-cutting factory. I regret that I did not buy a diamond, if only a very tiny one.

We enjoyed dinner at a little place where they spoke no English and was it fun! Using a combination of German, French and sign language, we managed to get something to eat. We fall into our beds now, entirely too late.

Date: August 20, 1938
Place: The Hague and Brussels, Belgium
Weather: Fine in morning, rain in p.m.

After breakfast, we joined a tour group for our train ride to Brussels. I was quite surprised at the size of Brussels. They say it has a million inhabitants. I certainly have a good opportunity to make use of my French, as they speak little else. Wanting to make the most of this afternoon in Brussels, we visited the majestic cathedrals, bustling market squares, and government buildings. We viewed many remnants of the German occupation of Brussels during the World War, and saw the place where Edith Cavell, a British nurse, was executed. She was charged with helping allied prisoners to escape.

Date: August 21, 1938
Place: Morning, Brussels and then on to Paris
Weather: Beautiful

Since today was Sunday, we were serenaded by the ringing of church bells. Our tour car ascended to the highest elevation in Brussels, which overlooks the old part of the city. The Palace of Justice here, is the largest building in the world and took over 21 years to construct.

After stopping to purchase some Belgian lace handkerchiefs, we drove by the Royal Conservatory of Music and the famous Mannekin Pis statue and fountain.

At a sidewalk café, we laughed until our sides hurt, as I struggled to order our lunch in French, *without being given a menu*! Soon after lunch, we headed for the train station and we were off to Paris!

France

Date: August 22, 1938
Place: Paris – tra la, tra la
Weather: Changeable – raining tonight

Tomorrow we will embark on a 3-day tour through Normandy, so the weather just has to be nice!

The Hotel Racine is on the left bank of the Seine in the Latin Quarter, right in the midst of the real French people. Our second floor room is enormous, with windows overlooking the street. People walk by or drive along, accompanied by the pleasant sound of tinkling bells which are the French equivalent of our blaring automobile horns.

French Touring Car of the 1930s

After a delicious lunch at the Voltaire Restaurant, we embarked on a tour of historical Paris, including the Arc de Triomphe commissioned by Napoleon in 1806. We drove by the huge Central Markets which are so vast that they overflow into the surrounding streets.

One has to see the Ile de la Cite, a natural island in the Seine. The island is home to many interesting buildings, particularly the Cathedral of Notre Dame. The rose windows of this cathedral date back to the 1200s and are especially beautiful.

We passed by the Louvre so often that it began to assume an old-friend air! We also viewed the Pantheon, burial place of famous statesmen and writers. After the tour, we found the cutest little beauty salon and had our hair washed and waved. We spent many pleasant hours, sitting in the Tuileries Gardens (the oldest park in the Paris) and the Luxembourg Gardens.

Sitting in the Tuileries Gardens with a portion of the Louvre in the background

Margy and I rode out to Montmartre and exited the bus at Place Blanche. To glimpse an overview of the area, we started wending our way up to the summit of the hill. We climbed street after street and step upon step, finally arriving at the Sacre Coeur Cathedral. Sacre Coeur is a comparatively new, all-white structure, which seems strikingly beautiful while soaring above its rather dirty surroundings.

After taking in the views from that high spot, we descended to what is called the Bohemian section of

Paris - Montmartre. We wandered for blocks amidst very narrow streets, which were thronged with people. The only reason that we didn't get lost, was our ability to see the Sacre Coeur Cathedral always towering above.

We were irresistibly drawn into a quaint little shop that offered etchings, watercolors, and prints. I made several purchases there, but wish I could have bought one of everything! While Margy completed her purchases, I became fascinated with a lively scene going on across the street.

The setting was an open-air café with people sitting around small tables, sipping wine. They were intently watching some performers who appeared to just step in from the street to add their bit to the show. The songs and dances were most unusual, to say the least!

The audience was not shy about letting their opinions be known. At the conclusion of each act, the performers were either rewarded with cheering and applause or they were met with the French equivalent of a loud "*Boo*!" We could have watched this scene for hours!

This was a part of Paris unlike any we had seen. The crowds were rough in appearance but seemed to be well behaved. Everywhere we went, the streets were teeming with sailors from the USS Nashville, wearing their crisp white hats. At a restaurant called No 7. Odeau Place, we found the steak and French fries to be cooked to the exact moment of perfection.

Chapter 4: France

Date: August 23, 1938
Place: Paris and Normandy
Weather: Rainy and fair - changing every half-hour

Our guide, Geoffe, called for us this morning in a smooth-riding Renault car. We sat with three other American women in the tour party who were quite arrogant and rude! I thought there was going to be a battle royal between them and us. Margy and I were so embarrassed by their actions and words that we felt like apologizing for them, to Geoffe! I now understand where foreigners sometimes get their unpleasant ideas of American tourists.

We rode by Versailles, catching enough of a glimpse to satisfy us until we return for a more leisurely visit. Our car cruised along through many large and small French towns. Lunch was enjoyed at the town of Alencon, a place known for its famous lace. I finally chose a handkerchief with one square inch of lace on it – it was just that expensive!

We drove straight on to Mont St. Michel in order to arrive an hour before it closed at 6 p.m. The rain very kindly ceased and our first glimpse of the Mont appeared against pale gray skies in the distance. The structure presents a stunning, unforgettable vision that resembles a castle out of a fairytale book - the sort of a place where a beautiful princess would be imprisoned.

We have a grand view with fresh sea breezes from the window in our fourth-floor room at the Hotel Poulard. What can be more relaxing than listening to the ocean? With so much to explore outside, it is difficult to stay in the room long enough to enjoy it. Shortly after our arrival, we left with a guide who positioned us so we could follow a French-speaking touring party. Our guide then spoke to us in English. It is impossible to describe the Mont fully! From the spire with the 8-foot tall figure of St. Michael, (450 feet above sea level) to the arched refectory, to the cloister with its dainty sandstone pillars, it is truly awe-inspiring. At one time, the Abbey was converted into a prison, but in 1863 the prison was closed. We visited the prison chambers, and touched the legendary chain. The legend goes, *"She who touches the chain will be married within a year."* All men beware!

Back at the Poulard Hotel, we watched a chef create the famous *Mere Poulard* omelettes and enjoyed a delicious meal, including omelettes and the famous salt grass fed lamb. The soufflé-like egg delights are oversized and quite fluffy. After dinner, we strolled the streets and made a few purchases. Our next stop is Normandy.

Date: August 24, 1938
Place: Normandy France (Trouville)
Weather: Absolutely perfect

What a lovely place to awaken in the morning! After breakfast, we drove through Avranches and right on to Bayuex, where we saw the famous tapestry in the library. Our guide explained the known history of the tapestry. It tells the story of William the Conqueror, and the invasion of England in 1066. It was thrilling to discover that I was able to read the entire story from the Latin that was woven or embroidered right into the tapestry. Of course, we all purchased printed copies of the tapestry so we can enjoy seeing it again and again. The car stopped for lunch at a hotel in Caen, where we recognized a French movie and stage actress who was seated two tables away. Her name is *Madeleine Renaud.* Miss Renaud graciously consented when Margy asked for her autograph.

We arrived at Deauville-Trouville about 4 p.m. Our guide said that Deauville is frequented by rich sugar daddies and their gold-diggers. We have been intently looking around to see some of them, but they have not crossed our paths. In spite of the crowds of visitors here, we managed to secure lovely rooms at the Langer hotel. As in Mont St Michel, one hates to be so plebian as to go to sleep. The area around our hotel reminds me of Atlantic City.

We sauntered along the boardwalk this afternoon, and then dove into large bowls of ice cream. Reclining under a boardwalk umbrella, we listened to divine gypsy music and gazed at people passing by. Dinner was followed by a visit to the casino, where we viewed gamblers play a roulette style game called La Boule. My one brave little gambling fling was unsuccessful, and I have no great desire to try again.

Helen and Margy at the Deauville beach

Date: August 25, 1938
Place: Normandy and back to Paris
Weather: Very good

It is difficult to plan our next Paris sightseeing tours, while shivering! The temperature must dip down to 50 degrees here in the evening, and there is no heat in our room. We had a lovely breakfast at the Hotel Langer, sitting in the terrace garden overlooking the sea. The food was delicious enough, but OH, how we enjoyed the apricot jam! Knowledge of the French language is essential in Normandy, especially when the guide is not with us. We drove to the Vieux Marche, to see the place where 19-year-old Jeanne d'Arc (Joan of Arc) was burned at the stake. Nearby is the spot where the tribunal sat in judgment, and a fine statue of Jeanne d'Arc. Dinner in Paris at the

Voltaire Café, and a walk on Rue St Michel, finished the day.

Date: August 26, 1930
Place: Paris
Weather: Fine

It is so grand to wake up in Paris, again! Poor Mr. Raffite is worried that we won't be going to an Apache nightclub. He has even offered to take us himself, the old darling. We will have to tell him when we decide to go, because they lock the hotel at midnight. If one plans to come back after midnight, he has to ask for a key to take with him. This morning we took the other part of our Paris tour, that of modern Paris, so-called. The crowded tour bus stopped at the Expiatory Chapel, which has been constructed over the burial place of victims of the guillotine – rich and poor - Marie Antoinette and Robespierre together.

Our drive down the Champs Elysees ended at the Triumphal Arch and the tomb of the Unknown Soldier, over which burns the eternal flame. The tomb was covered with lovely flowers, this morning. We noticed that there is a wonderful view from this Arch, across the Champs Elysees, past the Place De le Concorde, to the Louvre.

Our next stop was the tomb of Napoleon, which is surrounded by the only remaining old flags of that period. The list of the battles that he fought and won is inscribed on the floor. Also at this site, are the tombs of several of Napoleon's Generals.

On a street named Rue de la Paix, we eagerly descended upon a Transatco store, and sniffed so much perfume that we could taste it for hours! The prices were so reasonable that we purchased several bottles. Now - to get it home safely.

Date: August 27, 1938
Place: Paris
Weather: Fine

Today was a full day of shopping for souvenirs, theatre tickets, and excursions. We secured some excellent seats for the opera, "Salome." At the large department store, "Au Printemps," we again reverted to shopping. Eventually tearing ourselves away, we took a taxi to the travel agency to arrange for trips to Versailles and Chartres. Tickets for the night-tour of Paris were clutched in our hands and we could hardly wait!

After dinner, we went on the night tour of Paris, visiting clubs and cabarets. I sat on the bus with an English fellow, who was the perfect image of a young Duke of Windsor. His family, seated in front of us, kept peering around to make sure that their son was behaving!

At a strange little Turkish club, we sipped dark Turkish coffee and listened to bizarre, fast-paced music. A beautiful belly dancer snaked her way between the tables, stopping at ours for several minutes. Before we left, I purchased an ornate ring that was made in Algiers. How often does one have the opportunity to buy jewelry that contains a secret little poison compartment?

Our next stop was a nightclub in a very rough Apache area of the city. This establishment used weird lighting and sound effects, in an effort to simulate a thunderstorm. The effect was like the Fourth of July and Christmas, all rolled together. We were served tall glasses of mint lemonade, which was surprisingly delicious!

The next club was called "Le Neant" – a ghastly place! We sat there and drank nasty beer, while being surrounded by skulls and skeletons! It is hard to say which was more unsettling - the performances, or the pictures on the walls. I think that "Le Neant" means nothingness. I wanted desperately to get out of that place.

Finally, the tour proceeded to "Le Bal Tabarin," one of the ritziest nightclubs in Paris. The floorshow was over an hour long, and consisted of a wide variety of skits, daring acrobatics, and dances. Can Can dancers in colorful ruffled gowns, did their high kicks, adding cartwheels and splits. Beautiful girls rode a fancy carousel, which slowly ascended from beneath the stage floor. Other dancers descended from the ceiling!

We drank champagne, and watched women cavort around, wearing nothing but their imaginations. Thoroughly exhausted, we tumbled into bed at 4 a.m.

Date: August 28, 1938
Place: Paris
Weather: Very nice

After lunch in the Latin Quarter, Margy and I strolled down by the Seine, and stopped several times to investigate the wares of the many bouquinistes (booksellers.) Our destination was the Louvre. Once inside, it was thrilling to lay our eyes on such a great number of famous paintings, such as the Mona Lisa, and others by Titian, Botticelli, and Van Dyke. We sought out the "Winged Victory" and "The Gleaners." I made a note to return another day, especially to see the "Venus de Milo."

We relaxed in the splendor of the elaborate Tuileries Gardens and then hunted up the "Restaurant les Ministeres" where we enjoyed an inexpensive but delicious dinner. We are having such fun trying out the little restaurants in France, with occasional visits to the large ones. The eternal struggle with the language sometimes produces peculiar things to eat, but we do not mind one little bit. Overall, the food is delicious – much better than that we had in England.

Date: August 29, 1938
Place: Paris
Weather: Still fine

This was our morning for the Flea Market. At the Porte de Clignancourt, the stalls were lined up, row upon row. This open-air market suffered decidedly in contrast to the Caledonian market in London. It is sometimes referred to as the "rag market" and to us it seemed like nothing more than piles of junk. I have to admit that we do lack the connoisseur's art of recognizing valuable knick-knacks. Margy bought a darling blue and gold Limoges cup and saucer.

We wandered around the market until noon. Since we seemed to be accumulating little else but dirt and germs, we rounded up a bus and returned to town. It is strange how we feel we need to take taxis to our destinations, but we always find a bus that takes us back. After lunch at the *Pam Pam – Bar de la Paris*, we searched for the shop of a dressmaker, who had been recommended by a friend. Instead of being a dressmaker, this lady turned out to be an excellent modiste, (milliner) who was such a good saleslady that she talked me into buying a hat! I am crazy about this hat! The style of the veil is one that I have always longed for. This unplanned purchase, forces me to get out my list of things to buy in Paris, and cross off the word "Dress."

Margy wanted to look at a ring she saw in the window of a jewelry store on the Ave de l'Opera, and I came out with a ring, as well! It only cost 50y and is bee-oo-ti-ful. She succumbed to the lure of a lovely handkerchief, on our way to the Place de la Concorde.

We taxied to the Eiffel Tour and took an elevator to the highest platform, from which we could see for miles. The view towards the Trocadero was lovely, but the most spectacular sight was the glistening whiteness of the Sacre Coeur in the far distance. L'ascenseur (the elevator) which took us to the top of the "tour" (tower) was quite unusual. We kept transferring from one "cabine" to another. The cabines were little glass rooms that moved up and down via pulleys. I believe the tower is second only in height to the Empire State Building in NY City. Rumor is that they are planning to take down the Eiffel Tour in a year or two. It seems like such a shame.

At the Opera, we had grand velvet covered seats in a box for eight. This seating was only available because most Parisians are on holiday in August. The beautiful staircases and elaborately framed mirrors make it one of the most magnificent opera buildings in the world. We saw Salome, (the story of John the Baptist,) a Swan Dance, and an interpretive dance called Elvire. There is no such thing as a sensible bedtime these days!

Date: August 30, 1938
Place: Paris and Chartres
Weather: Cloudy, but fine.

Traveling from Paris to Chartres, we drove past the military camp in Satory, and caught a glimpse of several hundred soldiers involved in all kinds of activities. Just beyond the former Abby of Port-Royal, a tire on our car blew out! The poor chauffer had to struggle with the tire while we wandered around picking flowers.

The town of Chartres was once the site of Druidical worship. The greater part of the present church dates back to 1200-1400. The stained glass Rose Window is truly divine. There are four entrances to the Cathedral, which are distinct in structure and in meaning. I found the south entrance with its figures of "The Last Judgment" and the twelve apostles the most interesting of all.

The touring car wound its way back to Paris, arriving at 6:00. We dined once more at "Restaurant les Ministeres" and then hurried home to go to sleep early for once.

PS: A funny thing happened today! We had asked the tour company for our former guide, Geoffe, to accompany us on this trip. "Geoffe" we got, (we thought) but imagine our surprise when our guide "Joffe" told us he was a twin brother of Geoffe! I still cannot believe they are not the same person! I do think that Geoffe knew more about architecture, whereas this Joffe was better looking!
PPS: I love the bells on carts and bicycles here – they tinkle in a most harmonious manner.
PPPS: We saw many women washing their clothes in the river – it seems to be the custom.

Date: August 31, 1938
Place: Paris, Versailles, etc.
Weather: Cloudy and cool, but no rain

Our first stop was at Malmaison, which derived its name from the fact that it was a hospital for sick people, (mal) before the Palace was constructed. This was the favorite residence of Napoleon and Josephine. She continued to live here after they divorced. It later became the property of the French

Government. We viewed some of Josephine's dresses, Napoleon's hats, and his camp furniture.

At Versailles, we first visited the Grand Trianon Palace used by Louis XIV, XV and XVI. The rustic simplicity of the little farm of Marie Antoinette contained many small houses and stables. Here she loved to forget about the affairs of state and just enjoy herself. The temple of Eros and the lovely woods were particularly attractive.

The elegant Palace cost 40 million pounds, and the interior elegance can be summed up as a treasure trove of gold, crystal and art masterpieces. We visited the chapel where Louis XVI and Marie Antoinette were married.

The Gallery of Mirrors was the height of magnificence with its 17 huge wall length mirrors and 17 corresponding doors opening onto the terrace and the gardens. The Treaty of Versailles was signed here in 1919, after the World War. The gardens of the Versailles Palace consist of beautiful flowers, rows of statues, numerous wide terraces, and elaborate fountains. After returning through beautiful countryside to Paris, we dined at the newest Café Voltaire.

Date: September 1, 1938
Place: Paris
Weather: Fine
Timeline: Hitler demands that Czechoslovakia immediately concede the Sudetenland portion of its country to Germany

Today, our first visit was to the Conciergerie, which was the prison for those to be slain by the guillotine. Our French-speaking guide talked so distinctly that I had no trouble understanding him. It seems that the prisoners were of two classes – those who could pay for their rooms, and those who could not. The latter class was herded together in a long dark disagreeable cell.

Around the corner from the cell were the stairs leading up to the tribunal where all were judged. Subsequently, the prisoners went directly to the court and thence to the guillotine. We saw the cells that housed Marie Antoinette, Robespierre and others. In Marie's room, there was a special niche for the guards to stand – just opposite her dressing table, however she was allowed to have a screen for privacy. A chapel now contains all sorts of relics, including the guillotine knife, Marie Antoinette's chair, and the pinpricked note by which she attempted to escape.

Our next visit was to the Sainte Chappelle, which is all that is left of the old Palace of Justice. This beautiful 13th century church is a perfect example of Gothic architecture in Paris. The colors of the glass windows seem to penetrate your soul, producing a magical effect. These windows are carefully taken down in times of war, even though it takes years to put them back in place.

Back in Paris, we visited the Pantheon where we viewed the tombs of Rousseau, Victor Hugo, Voltaire, Zola, and others. We strolled through the

Luxembourg Gardens then shopped for cheap suitcases to hold our many purchases. The suitcases we bought are not much more than cardboard boxes with handles, but they will do.

We ended our afternoon at the Café de la Paris, sipping Dubonnet and watching the crowds throng by. They say if you sit here two hours, you will see someone you know. Our evening out included a lavishly produced show at the Folies Bergere. It was indeed an elaborate spectacle, which reminded me greatly of the Ziegfeld Follies – with a little more nudity. I think I enjoyed the Opera more.

Date: September 2, 1938
Place: Paris
Weather: Fine

After breakfast, a shopping excursion was followed by a visit to the American Embassy. We were to meet a Mr. Lester Mallory, to whom I had a letter of introduction. He took us to lunch at the famous Rougier Rotisserie. He ordered a strange mixture of lobster and fish, called Bouillabaisse, which is one of the typical dishes of Southern France. We also sipped wine from the South of France, and enjoyed a dessert of fruit compote in cognac.

It was an excellent lunch and Mr. Mallory made an interesting host. We parted at 3 p.m., so there was not much left of the afternoon. Of course, I made a special trip back to the Louvre to see the Venus de Milo. After dinner at Pam Pam, it is time to finish packing and so to bed.

FOLIES-BERGÈRE

Location du

TÉLÉPHONE

GALERIE 1re SÉRIE

No

PRIX	19.00
Timbre en compte avec le Trésor	0.25
Location	1.00
Total. . .	20.25

01204

Prière de conserver ce ticket pour être présenté à toute réquisition

Helen's ticket to the Folies-Bergere in Paris

Pontoon bridge on the Rhine River at Coblenz

Germany

Date: September 3, 1938
Place: Paris to Cologne
Weather: Fine

After saying good-bye to our nice little chambermaid, and Mr. Roffatti, we taxied over to the train for Cologne. Our basket lunch never materialized, so we nibbled on chocolate and made that do until dinner. We arrived in Koln (Cologne) at 5:30 and were happy to see our representative from the Eden Hotel. It is a lovely Hotel, situated near the station and the Cathedral. Everything seems so very clean here. We have what looks like a huge pillow all over the bottom portion of our bed. I have my legs tucked under it now and they are warm as can be.

We enjoyed a fine dinner at the hotel, which included steak, soup, and five vegetables. After dinner, we purchased a Rhine River Panorama booklet then walked along the banks of the Rhine. Tomorrow we take off for Coblenz by steamer boat.

Date: September 4, 1938
Place: Cologne to Coblenz
Weather: Fine, but definitely chilly

What a day! We left Cologne at 8:00 a.m. After getting our belongings settled, we sat down at one of the tables to enjoy our 6-½ hour Rhine River journey. The outdoor seating consisted solely of tables and chairs. Due to the chilly weather, most of the table tops soon contained cups of hot coffee for warming the passengers. We found one other English-speaking couple on the boat. There were flags of all countries at the tables, but since we were with our English friends, we sat under the British flag.

A mist hovered on the Rhine until after lunch, but nonetheless, the trip was captivating. We glided past Bonn, (Beethoven's birthplace,) in addition to many unpronounceable mountains and castles. Lunch was served in the dining room downstairs. The famous Rhine salmon was delicious! We are told that they are plentiful in this river.

There was a big party of German people having the best time. We have decided that we really like the Germans! They are most jovial, very polite, and the most cordial people of any country we have visited so far. By the time we arrived at the Riesen Furstenhof hotel in Coblenz, it was 4 p.m.

Our grand top-floor room faces the Rhine, with lovely vistas and a view of the *pontoon bridge* shifting to allow the boats to pass through. We never grew tired of watching sections of the bridge-on-boats move away and back again.

Coblenz is one of the places where American soldiers were stationed after the last war, so the citizens are somewhat accustomed to having English-speaking people around. Curiously, three little girls followed us on our stroll through the town, pointing their fingers at us and laughing. We walked up to the very imposing statue of Wilhelm I, on horseback, which was situated at the confluence of the Rhine. It is THE landmark of Coblenz, and can be seen silhouetted against the sky for miles around.

It was interesting to note the different colors of water at the confluence of the two rivers in Coblenz. The Moselle was tinted a much darker green than the Rhine.

After an excellent dinner at our hotel, with music by a German orchestra, we set out to meet our English friends (from the Rhine River ride,) at the bridge. We planned to walk together to the Weindorf Restaurant for some music and dancing. While we were waiting on the upper part of the bridge, four fellows came by and insisted that we go to the Weindorf with them! They would not take "No" for an answer! After I struggled with my English, German, French, and sign language to indicate that we were waiting for friends, two nearby English girls, conveyed our message. We thought things had settled down for a bit, until two drunks came staggering by and they scared us all over again. Since our other friends were late, we continued on to the Weindorf with the two new English friends, one of whom could speak German very well. We found a table outside and drank German champagne which tasted like cider.

The Weindorf turned out to have a party atmosphere and we had such fun! Handsome fellows would come up and stand before you, bow deeply, then click their heels and ask you to dance. You felt impelled to dance with them when they asked you in such a charming manner. It was the thing to do! They were excellent dancers – one and all! Some of the German musicians wore huge comical straw hats.

We sang at the table and we sang while dancing. The two English girls went home and left us with two fellows. Margy was with a blonde man named Helmut and I spent my time getting to know a dark-haired fellow called Toni. Helmut was really the best-looking man there but Toni had such romantic looking eyes. They wanted to take us home, but being a little wary of that, we declined.

We left there at 12:30 then discovered another place where we sipped coffee, danced again, and met two new fellows. Margy's friend, Wilhelm, could speak English fairly well. I had a quite a struggle talking to my new companion, Herman. He knew only 10 English words, but we still had lots of fun! Margy and I arrived home at the shocking hour of 4 a.m. It certainly did not take us long to fall into bed.

PS: It is hard to become accustomed to the way people keep looking at us. In the dining room this evening, it was almost comical to watch them stare when we were on the way out the door. They shall all have stiff necks tomorrow morning.

Date: September 5, 1938
Place: The Rhine – Coblenz to Heidelberg by steamer
Weather: Cold!

It was difficult to drag ourselves out of bed, but the boat to Mayence was due to leave at 10:15. Wilhelm was down at the dock to say goodbye and he brought some cough drops for Margy's throat. He really was quite sweet and thoughtful. Herman (the lazy thing) was still in bed and told Wilhelm to SEND his best wishes.

Today's steamer trip was not as pleasant as that of yesterday because it was uncomfortably cold with intermittent rain. Some people were wearing fur coats. We just sat and shivered. This journey was described as the most interesting part of the Rhine, offering stunning views of castles, the Lorelei Rock, and the haunting statue of her. One of the waiters pointed out the Lorelei Rock to us. He dashed upstairs to retrieve my camera. I rewarded him with some of my Lucky Strike Cigarettes, which I brought along to give away. As far as the rock goes, I could not exactly see the sirens combing their golden hair, but my imagination did a fairly good job of it.

The weather turned frigid, so we finally retired to the salon, where Margy slept and I read. The boat landed at Mayence at 6 p.m. We grabbed a taxi, and hurried across town, arriving at the railway station just in time to catch the train to Heidelberg. It was quite dark outside when our train arrived in Heidelberg, so we could not see much except the thousands of lights twinkling below our Hotel Schloss. We were met by the hotel bus and taken for a ride up the mountain, as they called it. Our hotel was at the very top, and the staff welcomed us as though they had just been sitting around all day waiting for our arrival.

We were escorted to our room, which was so large that we were almost got lost while walking from one end to the other. Our first – but very unromantic - impression of Heidelberg was one of blessed comfort! The room actually had heat! We clung to the radiator in delight. In no other place during this trip has that extraordinary phenomenon occurred. There is a balcony off our room from which we gazed down upon the brightly illumined river. The Neckar peacefully flowed under the old bridges. It was fortunate that we saw the beauty of the town by night, as the next morning it was pouring rain!

Again, we gave thanks for the heat. Rain or no rain, we wandered all over the town and environs, visiting the famous Heidelberg Castle. This huge building has been the victim of wars, fires (even a lightning bolt) yet is still an overwhelming sight. The rain somewhat dampened the romantic effect, but we called upon our ever-ready imaginations. We are in such a quiet hotel, and would love to stay here a week!

Chapter 5: Germany

Date: September 6, 1938
Place: Heidelberg to Nuremberg
Weather: Rain except at night
Timeline, September 6-12, (Nuremberg Rally) Hitler demands right of self-determination for the Sudetenland Germans.

Last night this place was so quiet that Margy and I slept as though we had been drugged. The hotel manager arranged for us to join a morning bus tour of the city. Although it was pouring, we managed to see quite a bit of the town, the University of Heidelberg, the odd road signs and the headquarters of the Student Prince. We journeyed alongside the Neckar River to the picturesque castle, which is now the home to concerts.

Margy and I left the tour party at the castle and wandered back over to our hotel. There was just enough time for a hurried luncheon before we headed for the railway station. My train was to depart for Nuremberg at 2:00 p.m. and her train was leaving for Freiberg at 2:30 p.m.

This was the scene of our planned parting, which prompted many hugs, well wishes, and quite a few tears. Margy will travel down through the Black Forest to Switzerland. She will then return to Paris and sail home on the Queen Mary. I felt terrible after leaving her and matters did not improve one bit.

In my train compartment sat four German soldiers, with poor little Helen squeezed into one corner! I was petrified because I thought all German soldiers were monsters or something. I was reluctant to move about, or even attempt to speak. The combination of being surrounded by soldiers in a smoke-filled compartment, and feeling bombarded with a constant flurry of German words, made me queasy – and things did not improve!

They never ran out of things to say! The soldier right next to me used the ashtray between us continually, letting his cigarette stub just sit there and burn. Upon arrival at the station in Nuremberg, I struggled to bring down my heavy suitcase but not one of them offered to help me! I was quite disgusted, still feeling a bit light-headed, and looking forward to getting some fresh air.

I departed the train amidst a swarm of military uniforms and managed to acquire a porter who hoisted my suitcase and carried it on his back. One could hardly walk in a straight line, as the street was filled with groups of soldiers, who were going in every direction. My suitcase-toting porter led me through the thronging crowds of men, to the Wittelsbach Hotel. I feared we would be separated, so I struggled to keep him constantly in sight!

Upon arrival in the hotel lobby, I received some devastating news! After the porter had dumped my suitcase and left, the desk man said that they had no place for me to stay! He said that they had notified my travel agency that there would be no room for me! I was completely flabbergasted! This was my first night without Margy, and I might have to sleep on a park bench!

While in Paris, I heard a rumor that Nuremberg hotels were turning people away if they were not on official business - even if they were offered large sums of money. That news had prompted me to check with the tourist office, where I was assured that the reservation was intact! Imagine my consternation! Judging by how many people were in town, I doubted that even a park bench would be available.

The desk clerk informed me that this was the beginning of the annual Nazi Party Rally. I just stood there aghast, hoping that somehow he would take pity on me and try to help. He picked up the phone and made a sincere effort to find a room in town, to no avail. When I felt I was about to collapse, he smiled slyly, pointed his finger upward, and said that he had a tiny room in the attic that was seldom used, but I could have it. I was so relieved! All I wanted at that point was a bed and a roof over my head!

The drab little attic room was freezing cold and had no running water - just a bowl and some ice-cold water in a pitcher! There was one window, which measured about one foot by two feet. It felt like I was imprisoned in one of those castle dungeons we had toured. However, I did have a roof over my head and I was not about to make any complaints to the desk. Instead of my hoped-for park bench, there was a bed, so I proceeded to flop down on it, and have a good cry. Thereupon, I felt much better! Isn't that feminine psychology for you? It appears that every time I get into a jam, somehow the situation turns out to be particularly exciting or interesting. Little did I know what lay ahead.

After I dried my eyes and powdered my face, I went downstairs to eat in the Bierstube. Like most places I had seen in Nuremberg, it was filled to the walls with soldiers. I crept to a small, unoccupied table in a dim corner of the room, and managed to get something to eat. Glancing cautiously around, I noticed that all of the other tables were occupied. Just then, a rotund German man holding a newspaper sat down with me. After we exchanged a few words, he decided his newspaper was more interesting than I was, so he hid behind it and continued to read. That was just fine with me, and I concentrated on my dinner.

Fortunately, he did not stay long. As I was about to leave, a couple of Austrian fellows wearing leather shorts, white socks and feathered hats, appeared. After their very polite "bitte" and my "ja, bitte" they sat down across from me. The atmosphere of excitement in the city made things seem informal, thus one of the Austrians began to talk to me. He soon realized that my command of the German language was not very good. After he had paraded his six or seven words of English, we had to get back to his mother tongue. The other fellow spoke nothing but German. Somehow, I got the point across that I could read and write German better than I could speak it, so we resorted to written conversations on napkins and paper scraps.

They were attending the Reich Congress, and proudly displayed their entrance tickets plus various newspaper clippings. In turn, I amused them with my passport and railway tickets. They were so easily entertained, and we laughed a lot. Visiting from their home town of Linz, Austria, they were in Nuremberg for the week. They seemed like such very nice boys. Max was the name of the tall light-haired fellow, and the shorter, darker man called himself Kurt. They wanted to teach me everything about uniforms, and pointed out variations in the room. I had to take notes on my napkin, or I would not have remembered it all!

It seems that some uniforms are not military, at all. There are a great many "politische" (political) uniforms, – which is the uniform in khaki - and it resembles our army dress. Then there are the "SS" who wear a similar uniform only of a dark color and with a different hat. The SA wear khaki uniforms, but with a different hat and band. The policemen usually wear dark uniforms with quite fancy hats. The true "militarische" (military) wear a strange colored grey-blue uniform and they customarily wear swords. Some fun, we had!

When I decided to leave, they begged me to stay while they finished eating. Since the idea of returning to that cold little room appealed to me not at all, I stayed on. After Max and Kurt finished dining, we walked through the streets, laughing, while trying to understand each other. The overall atmosphere in town was just like a carnival, with such merriment and general fun everywhere! Max asked if I would like to walk by the Hotel Kaiserjof -

where Hitler was staying - and of course, I agreed. As we grew nearer to the hotel, some military guards called out, and cautioned us to turn back. We could not get within a block of that building.

We gaily wandered the streets, as they pointed out the different uniforms we discussed at dinner. Back in the States, I never see a reference to the S.S. and the S.A. troops in the newspaper, but here I was, learning the difference first hand. We could not get into much of an argument on politics, because of our limited speaking abilities. We laughed and talked about simple things, which, I guess, was just as well. People kept staring at me. I think they wondered what kind of a uniform I was wearing. My dark blue ensemble was a sort of military-looking suit, with domed silver metal buttons and a matching cape. I must have intrigued people who were immersed in such a military atmosphere.

A group of young policemen from Hamburg, joined hands, sang, and danced in a circle around us. Max's translation of their words was "You are so lovely, you are so beautiful." The policemen only stopped their antics when their commander shouted an order for them to move on. Everything was in the spirit of celebration and gaiety, and the fellows acted so proud when anyone paid attention to me. Max and Kurt were both quite handsome. After they walked me back to my hotel, we finally had to say good night. They made me promise to be at my hotel at 11:00 a.m. tomorrow, when they will come for me and show me more of the sights. They tried to persuade me to stay over in Nuremberg, instead of going to

Munich tomorrow afternoon. I tried to explain that it was necessary for me to go. Kurt said he wanted to dance with me, and it was too late to do that tonight. Max inquired if I was engaged to be married, and when I answered "*No*," he solemnly said that he was not engaged. It is sad that I cannot stay over, because it would have been so much fun. Back now in my tiny cold room, it's hurry to bed before I freeze.

Date: September 7, 1938
Place: Nuremberg
Weather: Misty
Timeline: Because of Hitler's demands on Czechoslovakia, France announces a partial mobilization of its armed forces

OH, what a day! I wish I could do it all over again. After rising early, and with the help of some very strong coffee in the breakfast room, I was ready to explore my surroundings.

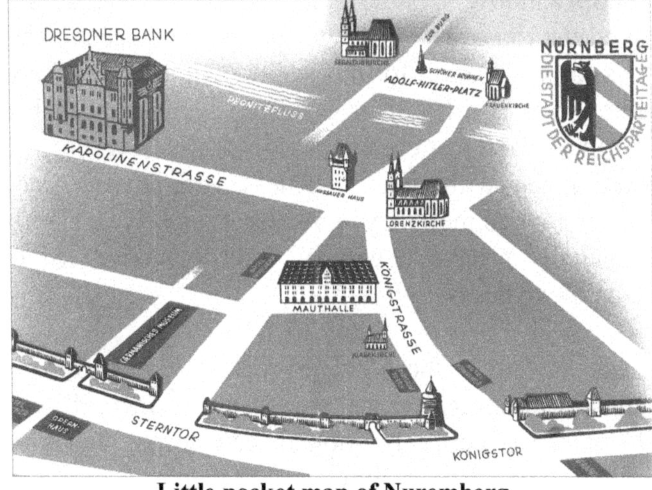

Little pocket map of Nuremberg

Despite the light rain, I wandered all over the old part of the city, visiting churches, public squares, and famous fountains. After climbing up to the Castle Schloss, I found the 600 foot deep Schloss well. To demonstrate how very deep it is, someone pours in six splashes of water. After the sixth pouring, you could hear the first splash hitting the water below. While taking out my wallet to pay my fee for this attraction, a handsome "militarische" stepped up and paid it for me! I feel like a regular gold-digger around here. The men will not let me pay for anything. A brief stop at the Rathaus revealed a costumed girls troupe who were marching and singing. There was a display of historical Nuremberg mementos in the upper level of the Rathaus. Nuremberg seems like a living museum of the Middle Ages. The town is decorated within an inch of its life. On the way home - while I was peering in a shop window - a fellow from Linz approached and asked me to go with him and his friend. It seems that it is quite proper to do such a thing over here, although it is difficult to adapt to being approached like that. Men just come up and ask if you want to go some place with them. Unless you have a good reason to decline, they consider themselves rightly offended! I have developed a little mental list of plausible excuses.

I was waiting in the hotel foyer at 11:00 when Max came dashing in, wearing a crisp uniform, if you please. He certainly looked handsome, and was thrilled when I told him so. Somehow, Max had secured for me, a ticket to the Hitler Congress! Along with Kurt, we took a waiting taxi out to the

Zeppelin Weise, (field) where I caught my first glimpse of the huge stadium.

Helen's ticket to the Congress – actual color is orange

I certainly would not have thought it possible, but we drove past all of the guards and police, and there we were - ready to exit our taxi and walk to the stadium! Our shoes became muddy, but we ploughed through it all, finally arriving at a place where we could look down into the enormous stadium. There was a golden swastika on the top of the seating section above the tribunal. Fires were burning in huge pots at either end.

I never saw so many uniforms of all descriptions, in my life! We viewed about 80,000 troops drilling on that one day. There were to be different troops marching on each day of the event. Max and Kurt's group would be reviewed on the following Friday. The thousands of people in the stands were cheering, waving, and shouting "Heil Hitler!" There was a most impressive marching ceremony before the Fuehrer arrived! It included all kinds of Companies and all sorts of people. Max, being a big strong, hefty brute, would lift me up when each new group of troops came on the field. I did not miss a thing!

There were bands of shirtless male youths called "Jugend," with spades in their hands. The youths were followed by troops of women, "Frauen" wearing dark skirts and white blouses. I heard that during one moment today, there were 40,000 people on the field and 300,000 in the stands. The cheering was deafening! Max explained to those around us, that I was an American. (In fact, everywhere we went people asked him about my nationality.) Judging from the expression on his face, he never tired of answering those kinds of questions.

Adolph Hitler arrived in an automobile and after taking his place, he delivered a short but emotional speech. A nearby man handed me his field glasses, through which I got a very clear glimpse of the Fuhrer. Hitler then listened to a thunderous series of heils, reviewed the marching troops, and quickly departed. When it was over, we strolled all around the Congress grounds, stopping for lunch at the Marine Building, one of the eating places designated for the troops. The building was teeming with soldiers. We had so much fun there. With great delight, Kurt ordered something for me, which he said was a delicacy. The waitress brought me a bowl of soup with a raw egg just dumped into it! I about died, but it finally went down. (Ugh!) We lingered there for quite a while, watching a floorshow, clicking glasses and eating strange things. The entertainment consisted of songs, music, and acrobatics, but most of my fun was centered on the fellows. I like them both, though Max is my special attraction. I have gone for him in a big way. He is so sweet - but then, so is Kurt.

All during lunch, the fellows tried to persuade me to stay over another night, and they kept overriding my excuses. Max even offered to find me a room, if my cubbyhole was no longer available. My resistance finally collapsed, and he telephoned the hotel to extend my stay.

Max and Kurt in front of the Maypole

After lunch, we again explored the grounds, and took some photos in front of the May Pole. The fellows took part in the usual carnival feats and games of skill. Max and Kurt did some shooting, which revealed that they are excellent marksmen! Kurt gave me one of his embossed silver military buttons, and I was really tickled by that.

Kurt's button

In the evening, we dined on schnitzel, potatoes, and vegetables, with brown bread. Dessert consisted of delicious Nuremberg Lebkuchen. The fellows drank beer, and after dinner ordered some wine for me, that I felt obliged to sip. Everyone sitting near us asked where I was from and why I was there. When the soldiers found out that I was from America, they would ask if I knew their Aunt Hilda or Uncle Otto in Chicago or New York. I became quite the expert at clicking my wine glass. After leaving that dining tent, we went to a larger tent building where we sang, linked arms, and danced around the table. Eventually, something I had eaten did not agree with me, for I felt quite ill. The fellows were so sympathetic that it made me like them even more. They walked me back to my hotel, and upon arrival, I felt much better. We sat in the hotel lobby talking and laughing until almost Midnight. Since they had to get up the next morning at 6:00, they departed after promising to return around 10:00 a.m. I hastened to my cold little bed. What a day!

Date: September 8, 1938
Place: Nuremberg and Munich
Weather: Sunny, thank goodness!
Timeline: British Inner Cabinet meets to discuss the crisis involving Czechoslovakia. They consider appeasement as a way of allowing time for British rearmament.

It wasn't until I looked at my wristwatch on the way down to breakfast, that I discovered the desk clerk woke me an hour early! I needed that extra time to pack because the fellows arrived a few minutes before 10:00. Incidentally, I am now depleted of the eight packages of cigarettes, I brought from America. Max and Kurt eagerly finished the last pack!

After a short stroll, we enjoyed coffee and rolls, then pushed our way through mobs of people, back to the hotel. It is so fortunate that I happen to be in Nuremberg at this time. It is possible to see a cross section of German life that I would never have encountered. People are here from every part of the country – a great many of them in their native dress. The stores are full of picturesque outfits. The girls look adorable, and the men's hats are adorned with piles of flowers and fluttering feathers. After returning to the hotel, we discovered that my bag had been taken to the station, so we wandered in that direction. The fellows bought platform tickets, so they could put me right on the train. We took more pictures with my little camera. How I hope they turn out all right. I promised to write and send my pictures and they did the same. In all too short of a time, the train arrived, and we had the dreadful job of saying goodbye.

Max and Kurt at the Nuremberg Train Station

Max removed an emblem pin from his shirt, and gave it to me. I felt very proud, as soldiers certainly hate to part with those.

1938 Nuremberg Rally emblem pin from Max

The train would not wait any longer, and I felt like crying when Max kissed my hand – oh dear! Though it seems to be a custom here, this was the first time that someone had ever kissed my hand. We waved good-bye until they were just specks in the distance.

Upon arrival in Munich, a porter asked the name of my hotel. He took my bag, however I lost him in the crowd. I finally found out where the hotel was, and sure enough - there sat my bag waiting for me. The hotel manager seems to be the only one who can speak English. Fortunately, my German speaking ability has improved considerably, due to conversing with Max and Kurt. Now I can make my needs known. In addition, my new German pocket dictionary will be of great assistance. It was too late to take any sightseeing trips in Munich, so after consulting with my map and guidebook, I walked all over town. I lingered in Konig Platz, a huge square over-run with doting mothers watching their gaily-playing children. Dinner at the hotel was a solitary affair, and I feel extremely let down, after all the fun of the last two days. The way Munich appeals to me now, I certainly am glad I stayed on in Nuremberg. Tonight, it's off to bed early, to recover some greatly needed sleep.

Max in front of the Maypole

Munich to Vienna

Date: September 9, 1938
Place: Munchen (Munich) toWien (Vienna)
Weather: A lovely day

Since I tarried in Nuremberg, I did not spend much time in Munich. After a quick breakfast – it was off again. This day included an eight-hour train ride to Vienna. Among my favorite features of foreign trains are the huge windows, which make it so easy to watch people and scenery. Consisting of one large glass pane, these windows can be raised and lowered with great speed. If you wish, you can stand in the aisle outside your compartment and gaze out of additional windows. When you arrive at a station, you do not carry your luggage off the train and hand it to the porter. You open a window - signal to a porter - then throw your bags out of the window! The trains do not stop for very long. Sometimes there is barely enough of an interlude to throw your bags out then run and jump out the door!

I shared my compartment with two old beret-wearing Germans, who both had such large bay windows they could hardly sit down. They looked like they must drink a lot of beer. They also spoke and read French so they must have come from near the frontier. They grunted to each other, read French newspapers, and dozed off, almost resting their heads on their huge stomachs. Craving companionship, I was dismayed at the idea of spending an entire day with these men.

Who should enter, but a nice looking German fellow, who sat down in the seat opposite mine. How long did it take for him to speak to me? It took two hours! After the silence was broken, we laughed at the way we had just sat and stared at each other.

Hubert said he was the headmaster at a military school in Berlin and he proved to be an interesting person. He spoke English much better than I spoke German, but sometimes we had to resort to both languages. My little English to German dictionary was now a big help.

Hubert on the train to Vienna

Whenever the train stopped, we opened the windows and hung our heads out to watch people at the stations. Both the men and women were wearing beautiful native costumes. At one stop, Hubert got off the train and purchased some delightful blue flowers – Alpenblumen - which he said, grew on nearby mountains.

The trip was a journey of stunning views, amidst mountains, forests, and lakes. As is the custom here, women were working in the fields. In those fields lay thousands of rocks topped with hay, which was drying in the sun. By and by, we entered Austria, where we stopped briefly in Linz. I sent the city a little kiss and took a photo for Max and Kurt. I certainly wish I could stop thinking of those fellows.

The ride was so long that by the end of the trip, we knew almost everything about each other. When our train reached Vienna, Hubert asked me to go to dinner with him. After I was all settled in my hotel, I dressed up for a change! We went by tram out to the famous "Rathauskeller" in the cellar of the Town Hall. The locals called it the "Rathaus." It was quite picturesque and very crowded. We ordered wiener schnitzel and drank the famous Grinzinger wine.

The resident orchestra included strolling musicians – a violinist and a singing accordion player who meandered throughout the audience. The music consisted of well-known Viennese waltzes and bits from operettas, which were thoroughly enjoyable. To my surprise, at one point they started playing "A Bicycle Built for Two," for my special benefit and for an English party at the next table. I sang it for Hubert, to his amusement.

We stayed there until rather late, and then we walked past the Maria Theresa Place. The statue of the Empress was impressive against a backdrop of the full moon behind her shoulders.

Near the Justice Building, we found a little coffee house, where we sipped sweet Viennese coffee, which was piled high with whipped cream. Here we listened to Hungarian music played on a cello, violin, and a xylophone-type instrument.

The house was not very crowded, so I had the thrill of being serenaded at our table. The musicians played with such feeling, it almost made me weep.

Hubert said that they were playing especially for me. He asked if I could feel the music in my soul, and that was exactly my experience. We were reluctant to leave, but it was quite late. After taking a taxi home, I said farewell to Hubert, for I was leaving early in the morning for Budapest and he was headed to Berlin. He was so very nice, but oh, Max!

Helen touring the Royal Palace in Budapest

Blue Danube and Hungary

Date: September 10, 1938
Place: On the Danube to Budapest
Weather: Fine – a little chilly

Instead of waiting to write a full diary entry this evening, I will add some thoughts this morning. It should be a rather uneventful day. The travel agent in Vienna did not think much of the twelve-hour trip down the Danube. The beautiful Blue Danube River was anything but blue, and it was not very beautiful when we started out.

I am half inclined to agree with the travel agent, but here I am, gliding down the Danube to Budapest! This boat is full of German and Hungarian natives and we are sailing under the Hungarian flag. It was necessary to go through customs before boarding, and to my surprise, the Customs Agents looked through my bags very carefully, this time! They poked fun by saying that some of my letters were probably from a sweetheart.

The officials here are quite intense about passports! I had to leave mine at the hotel for an hour, and relinquish it again today at customs. They said they would give it back to me, upon my leaving the boat. All this is most strange, but I guess they need to be careful.

There was a typical old Austrian man sitting next to me. His hair was as white as his collar, which was spick and span. He insisted on trying to talk, but he spoke a dialect that I could not understand. At noon, he brought out his little package of brown bread, sausage, and pungent-smelling cheese, then gulped it all down.

The Californian on board, turned out to be rather rude, and two English sisters were bored with everything! I enjoyed the company of a girl named Helga, from Danzig. (That is exactly how she autographed this diary.) She spoke some English and we were able to communicate beautifully. It was dusk when we neared Budapest. By this time I was becoming ecstatic about being on this boat trip. The final few miles were mesmerizing!

The reflection of the moon on the serene Danube, and the approaching lights of Budapest, created an incomparable romantic setting. Near the shoreline, adding to the dreamlike scene, were the black silhouettes of treetops, emerging from the water's surface. As we two swayed to the haunting strains of Hungarian music – wafting toward us from a radio - Helga and I exclaimed over the ever-changing panoramic views. All we could manage to say was "sunderschon" (gorgeous) over and over again! As we grew nearer to Budapest, we saw millions of lights – a spectacular display! Gazing up to the summits one could see (illuminated) the Citadel, the Parliament building, as well as churches and domes. We were totally enraptured, and wished it would never end.

Alas, the time was 8:45, and it had been a long journey. I sadly lost track of Helga somewhere at customs and the driver who was to transport me to my hotel, was nowhere to be found. Not wanting to go hotel-hunting in this land of strange words and signs, I hastened to a taxi, and had to pay the driver with Hungarian money borrowed from my hotel!

Before flopping in bed, which looked so inviting, I made arrangements for a trip to Mezokovesd, for tomorrow. Mezokovesd is a village outside of Budapest, where on Sundays the peasants put on their festival clothes, attend church and promenade around the square. I came directly to Budapest just so I could be here on a Sunday, and will return to Vienna later.

Date: September 11, 1938
Place: Budapest
Weather: Fine, but very windy

I reached the travel place by subway and was delighted to find several other English and Americans waiting for the tour.

During lunch at Mezokovesd, our small group was entertained by more of that captivating Hungarian music. The English-speaking folks in our group congregated around one table. Lunch consisted of sausage and cheese, with bread, fruit and tea or coffee.

On to the promenade! As planned, we climbed up into the balcony of the church and waited until it looked like the service was about to end. Then we tiptoed down and outside, so as not to miss the promenaders as they came out. Sure enough, we saw the girls walk around the square in front of the church, in the "Corso" as they call it. The young ladies joined hands in groups of two or three and strutted. The little boys looked so cute, spiffed up in their equally fancy suits. The colorful clothing was made up of multiple layers of fabric, lace, pleats, and petticoats for the girls. Some boys pointed, laughed, and made silly remarks about the girls. Ignoring the boys, the young ladies welcomed the opportunity to show off their beautiful, elaborate outfits.

When we stopped for coffee and cake on the way home, a Dutchman entertained our table with feats of magic. During a visit to one little village, we intermingled with some crazy wine festival revelers! Somehow, we became so caught up in the fun that we found ourselves marching with the natives in a long parade! Finally, realizing our bus was about to leave, we dashed back onto our bus laughing and dancing down the aisle to our seats.

At 8:00 p.m., I joined a group for a nightlife tour. At first, I was dismayed because I couldn't find another English-speaking person on the bus. As always, things turned out just fine! A friendly German man from Hamburg sort of attached himself to me, thus banishing my lonely feeling.

Budapest must be one of the most beautiful cities in the world at night, starting with the lights twinkling on the river. The buildings are illuminated at their bases with a lovely pale green hue which imparts a fairyland atmosphere to the whole scene. You are afraid to breathe for fear it will all disappear! We drove around the city then up to the Citadel for a higher view of the lights on the river.

Our second stop was at a small coffee and wine café which had a Hungarian orchestra. That visit put us in the mood for the Moulin Rouge, a charming nightclub just around the corner from my hotel. Here we danced the Tango, drank champagne, and watched an excellent floorshow. I surprised myself and did the Lambeth Walk like an old hand.

Music was being performed everywhere we went! Next to the door of each nightclub there was a saucer full of coins, with a sign that said "for the music."

After several more stops, the bus dropped me at my hotel at 2:15 a.m. Saying "Good Night" to everyone was difficult!

Date: September 12, 1938
Place: Budapest
Weather: Perfect

Arthur, the handsome young desk clerk, invited me see the Gypsy Boys orchestra at the Café Ostende this evening. Having heard so many wonderful things about this group, I was delighted at the thought of seeing them in person! This morning, he told a porter to accompany me to the subway that went to the tour office. They suggested the three-hour express tour, which was about to leave. In order to see Budapest and the Blue Danube from above, we drove up to the Fishermen's parapet. The seven towers symbolize the seven Magyar tribes that arrived in Hungary in 896.

The Turks have so often overridden Hungary that their traces are everywhere, beginning with an odd mixture of Turkish and Gothic architecture. We visited the famous Gellert Thermal Baths, which opened in 1918

.

We were invited to take a peek at the wave pool, where artificial waves are generated by a mechanical device at one end of the pool. Bathers seemed to enjoy standing in this pool, trying not to get tipped over when a wave came upon them. Unfortunately, there wasn't time to take a swim. Budapest contains many of these health-giving thermal baths. The natural temperature of the water is quite hot, and when brought inside a building, it heats up a room.

Helen with tour group at the St. Gellert Baths

After lunch, I walked down to the park in front of the National Theatre where the peasants were selling their wares. The money I brought along was dwindling so I had to be satisfied with a black belt decorated with red and green embroidered Hungarian designs. After getting lost two or three times on the way back to the hotel, I indulged in a short nap before my date with Arthur, at the Café Ostende.

It was a lovely evening, illuminated by a nearly full moon. We arrived at the Café Ostende just as the adult orchestra was playing their last piece, which preceded the Gypsy Boys show. The boys orchestra was splendid! Wearing elaborate costumes, some of the tiny tots seemed almost too small to hold a violin! There was not one sheet of music between them! That is the way with musicians in all of Hungary. I was informed that they play more by ear, than by memory. Some of the older boys played larger instruments, however they all looked of school age. We loved every moment, and wished it would never end.

After an intermission, the adult orchestra resumed their playing. We had a grand table right in front of the stage. Arthur was well acquainted with both the manager and the orchestra leader. The leader, a gypsy king, eventually came down to speak with us. He said I am a nice girl and that I should stay in Budapest and take care of Arthur. He also told me that I was not a real American because I seemed too romantic. I am not sure of the reason for that statement, but I do love to close my eyes and sway to the Hungarian music!

The manager spoke English well and interpreted the Hungarian gypsy songs for us. He came to our table, sidled up to me with a violin tucked under his chin, and gazed soulfully into my eyes. Although this is common in the nightclubs here, I still found it quite flattering. (However, if it carries on too long, it feels a bit unsettling.)

Arthur and I sipped wine and became more and more entranced with one another. He transformed into quite the romantic lover, and begged me to stay in Budapest and marry him! It is fortunate that the music ended when it did. The situation was becoming quite treacherous. We were the last ones to leave Café Ostende.

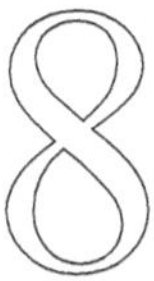

Austria

Date: September 13, 1938
Place: Budapest to Wien
Weather: Overcast but no rain
Timeline: Marshall Law is declared in the Sudetenland, by Czechoslovakian President Benes.

Up early again! This is too much! My train was scheduled to leave at 8:30. Arthur ordered breakfast and helped me close my bag. I longed to extend my stay in Budapest. I do not know why, but having my hand kissed makes me feel so sentimental. Perhaps it is because men do not kiss our hands, in America. A great many soldiers down at the station were marching and drilling, but everything seemed peaceful enough. I kissed Arthur good-bye, climbed aboard the train, and was off for Wien. (Vienna)

A driver, from the travel service in Wien, met me at the station, and described several sightseeing tours.

He also stated that they have been darkening portions of the city at night in preparation for possible air raids. On the way to the hotel, I was dismayed by his stories of the black nights they had experienced, with all lights out and not a glimmer of shine, anywhere. It sounded like it would be terrifying, especially if one was a tourist unfamiliar with her surroundings.

Well, Dear Diary, all of the late hours and irregular meals caught up with me here in Vienna, where I am planning to stay several days. I became so sick that it was necessary for the hotel to call a doctor. He said that it was nothing to be alarmed about, but still ordered me to stay in bed for 2 days! I am too frightened to disobey his orders! My day was filled with periods of sleeping and waking. I am not sleeping soundly because of the clamor outside! The window in my room is vibrating from the sounds of soldiers marching by!

Date: September 14, 1938
Place: Vienna
Weather: Sunny

I am snuggled up in my bed, still resting, and slowly recovering. Although my desires are to be out doing things, my body does not want to cooperate. There was so much excitement in the street today! There were parades with bands and troops marching by, people laughing and talking, and streetcars jingling their funny little bells. I am sure I shall feel well enough to participate in the morning. If I had to be sick somewhere, I am glad it was here in Vienna where I am spending 3 1/2 days.

Late this evening, what seemed like 10,000 soldiers - interspersed with drummers - marched by, drowning out all other noise! The banging of the drums reverberated off the buildings. The marchers were shouting, chanting and singing! They were coming from the direction of the Westbahnhof Railway Station, which is not far from my hotel. I peeked between the curtains and watched them stream by until the whole spectacle made me dizzy! I tumbled back into bed!

Date: September 15, 1938
Place: Vienna
Weather: Rainy
Timeline: the crisis impels Great Britain's Neville Chamberlain to fly to Germany for a meeting with Hitler.

Learning my lesson about the necessity of sleep, it was not until this afternoon that I felt like venturing out with a tour group. Vienna is particularly interesting as the home of so many great musicians. There are monuments and remembrances everywhere to Strauss, Schubert, Brahms, Haydn, Mozart, and Beethoven. The scheduled afternoon tour took us past the houses where many famous musicians lived and worked: where Schubert wrote "Blossom Time," and Beethoven his "Eroica Symphony." We passed through the famous wine suburb of Grinzing. If you see green flags hanging in front of a house, it indicates that the owners have their own fresh wine for sale. This is the greatest wine growing district of Austria. It was so cold and windy that we did not tarry long.

We were served lunch on a mountaintop near Leopoldsberg. Seated around tables in a glass walled room, we enjoyed the spectacular view along with our delicious Viennese coffee. The drive home took us past Schubert's birthplace and the Opera house. It is still raining, so off to bed, early!

Date: September 16, 1938
Place: Vienna
Weather: Cold!
Timeline: British Lord Runcamin recommends that Czechoslovakia border territories containing a majority of ethnic Germans, be relinquished to Germany

The sun shines bravely through the cold weather. The tour man said to expect snow in Switzerland. I think I will go shopping for a hot water bottle! This has been an easy day.

In my rambles about town, I did observe something unique. In almost every shop window, I saw red stickers saying either that it was an "Aryan store" or a "Party store." Some stickers said, "Approved by the Arbeits Party." There were gas masks in almost every store window display! Next to each gas mask stood a poster that read: "I have mine; do you have yours?"

There were signs posted everywhere, indicating that one could find "cellar rooms" nearby. A cellar room was to be sought out, in the event of an air raid. These shelters must have been numerous because no matter where one stood, they could see at least one sign that indicated how many minutes to a particular cellar room, and the number of people it could hold.

Looking around for evidence of activity against the Jews, I did notice one large terrible picture of a Jew - with long grasping arms - holding churches, schools, and banks. There were many evidences of an unsettled state. The streets - and even the houses - were teeming with soldiers.

Here in Vienna, they surely believe in preparedness. It seems they are going to have four "black nights" next week, and I shall miss them all.

A special event that I would like to have seen, is the changing of traffic from the left-hand side of the street to the right-hand side, in accordance with German custom. Vienna is the last Austrian city to change over. This is to take place tonight at midnight. I need to leave town early tomorrow, so I they will have to perform the ceremony without me. It has been interesting watching them change the streetcar entrances, all in preparation for the stroke of midnight. I came back to the hotel for lunch and to rest, as tonight it will be rather late when I return.

Our Vienna night tour was wonderful! I met only two English-speaking people, but there were others who tried to speak it. We went to the Prather amusement park and rode on the famous Ferris wheel and the scenic railway. This is a huge amusement park along the Viennese lines of a Coney Island. The roller coaster seemed tame compared to those in America. On the way up to Koblenz, we drove by

Schubert's birthplace. The air was very clear and chilly, but we had a lovely view of Vienna and the Blue Danube by night. We then visited the Koblenz Bar, where an orchestra alternated between Viennese music and American Jazz. One minute we heard the Blue Danube Waltz, and the next tune was Billie Holiday's "Says My Heart."

The Germans drank American cocktails while the Americans and British enjoyed German champagne. Our next stop was at Grinzing where we were lead down into a cellar to learn how wine is made. After tasting several types of wine, we returned to the main level, where we sat around tables, eating strange things on rolls and drinking wine. Here we enjoyed an excellent orchestra with musicians who wandered among us. During the last melody, we sang, joined hands, and swayed around the table. On our return trip, it was comical to see the transformation of the people on that bus. Everyone was having a good time - singing and laughing - even the stout old ladies. When the bus dropped me off at my hotel, it was difficult to tear myself away from that party. They probably kept it up until morning. I had to arise at 6:30, so I trotted off to bed like a good little girl.

Date: September 17, 1938
Place: Vienna to Salzburg
Weather: Wunderschon

This has been another one of those days fraught with surprises. The Budapest to Paris train left Vienna a little after 8 a.m. and most everyone else was going farther than Salzburg. The atmosphere seemed very stiff in our compartment at first, so I sat and read a detective story. The man across from me (who had been dying to talk for the last hour or so) broke down and spoke some English. From then on things were better. Three fellows boarded shortly after we passed Linz. They carried a portable radio, so we skimmed along, listening to some of the prettiest Viennese music.

The newcomers spoke about ten words of English, and they turned out to be lots of fun. I almost died giggling at the youngest fellow's imitation of a Spanish dancer. He had the fair hair and blue eyes that so many of these Austrians possess. They all reminded me of Max, unfortunately.

As we approached Salzburg, the countryside was studded with sparkling blue lakes against a background of heavenly snow-capped mountains. I was still entranced upon my arrival at Salzburg, and thus unprepared for the shock that lay ahead.

After departing the train, I looked for my baggage, but it was nowhere in sight! I tried desperately to find my way to the street. Usually when I exited a train, I just followed the crowd. This time there were very few people, and they had scattered in all directions. After many false turns, I emerged at the street, and found my baggage sitting there, with no one around.

When I asked a taxi driver to go to the Salzberger Hof Hotel, he said that it had not been a hotel since the German occupation of Austria, the preceding

March. It was now a German military headquarters! I carried a book of prepaid coupons with which to pay for all of my hotels. You can imagine my consternation at having to spend some of my precious German marks (which I needed for purchases) on a hotel bill. I had planned it so that I would not have much money left over, as one can only take 10 Marks out of the country. Since I was leaving the country right after my next stop at Innsbruck, I was in a pretty picklement.

After being shoved from one place to another, it finally turned out that I would have to pay the hotel bill myself, for these two nights. The penny-counting really intensifies now. A clerk at the railway station said I had better go to the Salzburger Hof anyway, and ask if they knew of a room. I stepped up into a horse-drawn carriage, commandeered by a big fat, mustached Austrian. He was extremely good-natured, spoke not a word of English, but proceeded to the Salzburger Hof. It was a lovely day, in such a lovely place, and I should have enjoyed it more if I had not been worried about having a place to stay.

Sure enough, my scheduled hotel was a military establishment, and it was occupied by Germans, not Austrians. I reported my dilemma to a kind female employee, who told me to follow her. She led me to Nazi Headquarters! (I guess I really reported it good, didn't I!) An official at Nazi Headquarters suggested I return to the railway station and find the tourist information office. I had another picturesque ride in the same little horse-drawn carriage.

The agent at the tourist information office secured an inexpensive room for me at the Elizabeth Station. It is near the railway station, and is close to many places of interest. My entire trotting around in the horse and carriage cost me only 3M, which was very reasonable. The jolly old driver had made himself available to me for at least an hour.

My lovely room is spacious, and decorated all in white. There is a wonderful view from the window and the quietness outside my room is refreshing. The jovial landlady actually speaks excellent English!

After checking my travel literature to see where things were located, I went for a walk in this most picturesque of picturesque towns. The tourist season is almost over, so there were few foreigners around. I sat in parks in the chilly air, and let the sun soak through me.

Salzburg is the most unique city I have seen so far. The native Austrian dress is the rule rather than the exception, although many of the men are wearing military uniforms. The women's dresses are so unique, that I long for the money and an excuse to buy one. How does one take photos of the gaily-costumed people, without seeming rude? Just as my travel book stated, the Salzburg men seem very friendly and romantic at heart.

Salzburg: River Salzach

The lovely River Salzach runs right thorough the center of the town, which is bordered on both sides by hills and mountains. I hear that the old fortress is filled to overflowing with Nazi troops.

Salzburg is a town of music. A foreigner visiting here is fully aware of it. There are mementos of Mozart all over town, including a statue, a bridge, and the home of his parents.

I stopped at a café house for some coffee and cakes, as a much-delayed luncheon, and then wandered to the Kurhaus – the Mirabell Schloss (Palace) and the peaceful Mirabell gardens. The sun was shining brightly and everyone seemed so happy and carefree. It was a joy just to wander in and out, by fountains and shady paths, past children playing and artists painting pictures. Almost everyone stared at me, especially the children. It is probably because of my military-style suit, once more.

Entrance to the Mirabell Gardens

My eyes are tired from trying to take it all in. At my hotel, I have arranged for "half pension" (that is, a room with breakfast and dinner.) At 8 p.m., I will descend the stairs, to dine at the "Speisesalle."

Date: September 18, 1938
Place: Salzburg
Weather: Noch Wunderschon
Timeline: There is a meeting in London, where British and French Cabinet members finalize an Anglo-French plan designed to appease Hitler with regard to the Sudetenland. Italy states that they will side with Germany if war breaks out.

What a glorious day! Despite feeling a bit tired, I did not hesitate to rise for breakfast in the Speisesalle with two darling little waitresses running all around. The tour bus picked us up in front of the hotel at 8:45 a.m., and by 9:00 a.m., we were reassembled at the agency for various tours. Today's excursion included visiting famous places in the city plus the Hellbrunn Castle.

We drove through the Residenzplatz, a large square in the historic center of Salzburg. After viewing the riding school, State Theater, and a tower where they used to burn witches, we ended up at the Hellbrunn Castle. This place is famous for viewing the many fascinating waterworks, which delight adults and children alike! Miniature carved people in miniature villages suddenly become animated, by the power of water alone. Water would suddenly spout from everywhere! There was a table surrounded by seats with little holes in their centers. The person at the head of the table could press buttons that would cause a spray of water to rise in the center of each seat - an easy way of ridding oneself of an unwelcome guest.

We arrived at the Residenzplatz just in time to hear the carillon play at 11:00. Our guide said it was a sad song that asked the question, "Why do you go away and leave me?" The cute little guide had a round, beaming face, and wore a Tyrol costume. After the tour, I revisited the lovely Mirabel gardens, just sitting there drinking in the sun. How many things could I squeeze into the remaining hours of the day? In the old part of town, I encountered St. Peter's Cathedral as they were having an organ recital. The organ dates back in part to 1628 and the music was magnificent. While making my way through the narrow streets, the entrance to the fortress, or "festung" appeared. I ascended on a cable car, which was somehow propelled by water. Sitting at the top of the hill, savoring my coffee and kucken, I had a lovely view out over Salzburg. The fortress seemed like a little village, and was teeming with soldiers.

Salzburg Fortress

Always looking for things to explore, I tried to find out where everyone seemed to be heading. They were going to the Herbfeste, a type of carnival. On the way down, I longed for a parachute that would deliver me right in the middle of the gaiety. After a lengthy and tiresome descent, I walked out to the Herbfeste. These Austrian people really are gay and I love them all! They enjoy everything immensely, and are so kind at heart. I would have enjoyed the fest even more with a companion. Carnivals are meant to be enjoyed with others. After exploring it completely, I could barely crawl back to my hotel.

The hotel dinner was quite refreshing, so I was ready to take in a performance of the celebrated Salzburg Marionettes. They acted out a very amusing rendition of Faust, and are every bit as wonderful as claimed.

Date: September 19, 1938
Place: Salzburg to Innsbruck
Weather: Grand

The ride from Salzburg to Innsbruck was completely entrancing: high rugged mountains rising on both sides of the road, many of them with snow-covered peaks. The mountain streams were as clear as can be! The river had an aquamarine hue, sparkling like strands of diamonds as it caught the sunlight. Initially, I had the compartment to myself and I hopped from window to window to see everything. Around every curve was another lovely lake! The people working in the fields wore a plainer version of the Tyrol costume.

Eventually, a very handsome fellow entered the compartment. He spoke little English but indicated that he was sorry that he could not get off at Innsbruck to show me around. He kissed my hand when he left at *Zell am See.* For the remainder of the ride, just curling up and enjoying the scenery far outweighed any desire to read or take a nap.

Upon my 2 p.m. arrival at Innsbruck, I went by horse and carriage to my hotel. The ride was enjoyable this time, with no worries about having place to stay. My room is lovely, and very well furnished. I am dying to try the bed – and had better do so early, because tomorrow morning, it's up at 6:30. This afternoon I walked around Innsbruck and visited the Folk Museum, to see some very old Tyrolean artifacts. There were costumes from all parts of the country, as well as various implements and furniture. Several men were in charge of the displays, and each was happy to show people the things in his particular domain.

That afternoon when I returned to my hotel room, I noticed that there was a contraption on the ceiling light – a sort of cardboard box - with a small hole in the bottom. When the light was turned on, all the illumination I could see was a small cylindrical shaft that was barely noticeable. My first impulse was to wonder what kind of game it was! It was then that I became aware that the windows were locked, and the outside shutters seemed nailed tight. After resting, I turned on the light over the washbasin and readied for dinner. During dinner in the hotel basement, I temporarily forgot about it all.

The dinner was delicious, but the other diners did not care to socialize. They were extremely engrossed in some news flashes that were blaring over a radio. I could make out what seemed to be a Sudeten-German mass meeting with several speeches and lots of wild cheering. The atmosphere was so intense that I felt the need to step outside for some fresh air.

The desk clerks in the dim lobby confirmed that this was a black night. When I told them that I had turned on the light over the basin, they looked aghast! Why didn't anyone tell me about this? The scene outside of the hotel was black as black could be. You could not see two feet ahead of you. It was a blackout night, all right! People were cautiously walking down the streets. They were speaking in hushed tones, and muttering to companions or to themselves!

It was the weirdest sensation – like being in a dream. It did not seem wise to venture far from the hotel. There were only two things one could do on such an evening: go to some nightclub to pass the hours, or go home and to bed.

Upon re-entering the hotel, I had a terrible time finding my room! The lights in the hallways were so dim that I had to grope each door and run my fingers over the raised numbers. More fun! After finally locating my room, I headed straight to bed, and slept like a top.

Lucerne Switzerland Lion Monument

Switzerland

Date: September 20, 1938
Place: Innsbruck to Lucerne, Switzerland
Weather: Still fine
Timeline: Officials of France and England inform Czechoslovakia that they will not help (if attacked) if they do not accept the French-Anglo appeasement plan. Czechoslovakia feels forced to back down.

While waiting for my taxi this morning, I met some American tourists who described their terrible sleepless night! They said they were kept awake by the sounds of troops marching all night, in addition to airplanes flying around! They feared there was going to be a battle right there and then, and were extremely dismayed. I, on the other hand, never heard a thing! There is one advantage to being overly tired. You sleep through all sorts of noise and escape some of those anxious moments that light sleepers experience.

My taxi departed the hotel about 7:00 this morning to catch a 7:20 train. The cab ran out of gas before reaching the railway station. It was too early to find another taxi, and as I could make out the station in the distance, I started running and told the driver to follow with my bags. Fortunately, the train was late in arriving so all was fine.

Again, the combination of beautiful scenery and congenial conversation kept me alert. I met a couple of lively American fellows. They were tall and handsome Cornell boys who will be staying in Zurich before going on to Lucerne. Resting up from the previous night in Innsbruck, they had selected the "nightclub method" of outlasting the blackout and ended up having a rip-roaring time. The fellow next to me was a seasoned traveler but he must be Jewish because the customs officials put him through the third degree.

The trip to Lucerne continued to be beautiful. Switzerland is as lovely as expected. It was a joy to see an agent waiting to greet me. I almost kissed him! After all of my recent hotel troubles it was grand to be looked after once again.

My hotel room overlooks the Lake Lucerne, with mountains in the distance. The tempting view from my little balcony keeps me from accomplishing anything when in my room. The travel man came to the hotel and we planned my stay here in Lucerne. We scheduled a mountain trip for the next day. I had the afternoon to myself to explore the city.

Lake Lucerne view from hotel

After walking all over town, I found the carving of the Lion, chiseled out of natural rock. It is such a kindly sad-looking lion. Looking at him almost gives you a lump in the throat – which is what the artist intended, I do think. The lion is a monument to the hundreds of Swiss Guards who were massacred during the French Revolution, in 1792.

The shops are filled with fascinating, albeit expensive items. The dresses that I admired cost about $30 each! I marveled at the old wooden covered bridges with their painted pictures. It is fun to walk cross the river again and again on different bridges, to see all the pictures. The "Dance of Death" bridge is one of the most interesting. In all the scenes, the figure of Death is represented by a skeleton.

It was quite late by this time so I returned to the hotel for dinner. The people here seem to do everything possible to make one's stay a pleasant one.

Date: September 21, 1938
Place: Lucerne
Weather: Fine

It was with the greatest pleasure that I remained in bed until 8:30. After breakfast I took another walk through the city and made several purchases based on yesterday's window-shopping. After lunch at a little coffee shop, I sat on a lakeside bench to write post cards before my afternoon trip. The sun made the sparkling blue water appear like a sea of precious gems. The clouds in the blue sky framed the snow-capped Alps.

Back in the hotel lobby, the desk clerk handed me a telegram from home. It read, "Please come home soon. Have you any idea what is going on over there? Love, Mother and Dad." I responded with loving assurance that I would be sailing home in just a few days.

The trip to Bergenstock was a new type of experience. We boarded a boat from the dock in front of the railway station. The 45-minute ride was delightful. Upon landing, we took a short funicular ride up the mountain Bergenstock. By this time I had become acquainted with a Canadian woman so I did not have to travel alone. She had been here previously and really knew her way around. We were rather amused to find out that we were not only both going back on the Queen Mary together, but her cabin is No. 133 and mine is No. 137! She is the first prospective traveling companion I have met. It was heavenly up on the mountaintop where rested three lovely hotels! Now I have a place to spend my honeymoon - and I even picked out the room!

We walked around, trying to find words grand enough to describe the sweeping vistas. After tea on the summit, we descended via the funicular to another boat ride, then back to our various hotels. I reached home in time to glimpse a stunning sunset with a breath-taking pink tinted sky. I am ready to fall into bed.

Date: September 22, 1938
Place: Lucerne to Interlaken
Weather: 95% perfect
Timeline: A new Czechoslovakian government is formed. Chamberlain meets with Hitler to discuss his demands.

"95% perfect!" That is what the guide said about the weather. What a day it has been!

They called for me in a Cooks Tour bus at 7:45 and after making just one more stop, we were on our way. The ride continued alongside the Regi Mountains and around about the Lake of The Four Cantons (Lucerne.) It is impossible to describe the splendor, the wonder, and the beauty of the panoramic views. The superb roads and railway lines are such grand feats of engineering! We passed through William Tell country and saw the place where he shot an apple from his son's head.

The journey took us up and down mountains, on narrow curving roads. Just when we thought the bus driver could not complete a hairpin turn, he did so perfectly! He navigated the bus through numerous breath-taking curves but never moved an eyelash. Some of the passengers became jittery after just so much of it. These Swiss drivers must have nerves of iron.

We saw hundreds of soldiers near the roads. We drove up eight thousand feet to the Furka Pass, where we had lunch. A couple of Swiss musicians entertained us with their singing and yodeling. Before moving on, some of us picked Alpine flowers.

We descended the mountain, only to climb back up again to see the marvelous blue white Rhone Glacier. Such a sight is hard to comprehend or to describe. The bus driver stopped at the town of Meiringen for tea. At this point, I boarded a bus for Interlaken, and the others returned to Lucerne.

Rhone Glacier: tourists in the lower right hand corner

In Interlaken, the busman said that my anticipated Hotel Bristol was closed for the season but that some other place had my reservation! He very kindly took me all around until we found the hotel that was expecting me.

I had only been in my room ten minutes when I glanced out of a window and behold - the clouds had parted! There was the Jungfrau in all of its white glory! The lovely vision of shining whiteness with a faint pinkish cast appeared for a minute or two. The views of the Jungfrau are just like that – visible for a moment, and then hidden behind clouds once more. Tomorrow – if the weather continues fine – I am going to take a trip up to the top. Just the thought of it thrills me to death. After a delicious dinner, I skimmed through an American magazine here at the hotel. I just cannot wait to tumble into my comfortable white bed.

Date: September 23, 1938
Place: Interlaken
Weather: Continued perfect
Timeline: Czechoslovakian government mobilizes its army.

Today has been a perfect day with a perfect trip to the Jungfrau. As an old shopkeeper said to me tonight, seldom has there ever been such absolutely perfect weather for this trip. The awe-inspiring feeling of being in the Alps defies description!

We took a train to Lauterbrunnen then switched to a train for Kleine Scheidegg. In speechless wonder, we drank in the beauty of pine-covered mountains where crystal clear streams tumbled downward in miniature waterfalls. After passing by small Alpine villages, we were transported via steep cog railway, which ascended through a long tunnel up to Jungfraujoch! The railway through the tunnel is a grand feat of engineering.

Having wondered how it would feel at 12,000 feet above sea level, I discovered that (except for a little shortness of breath after climbing steps) all was fine. It was absolutely necessary to wear dark glasses because of the bright sun however its warmth kept us from feeling too cold.

We rented some "snowshoes" which turned out to be high galoshes, and went plowing out into an entirely new world – all ice and snow. There was nothing but a wonderful feeling of freshness and isolation from the rest of the world. Everything was blanketed with extremely deep snow. We tramped around and admired the beautiful views below. Perched high on a peak, we enjoyed our box lunches, gazing off into unbelievable splendor.

View from the top of the Jungfrau

Now it was time to play! After visiting the blue-green ice palace, I sat on a sled on the ice rink while a handsome fellow twirled me around and around. Of course, this all ended with a snowball battle!
Some of the folks went skiing, but I preferred to spend the time on other sports.

Exploring the Jungfrau

A group wanted to see the polar dogs so I tagged along. We descended on foot, and suddenly my left leg went all the way down through the snow bank! It was the strangest feeling!

At the enthusiastic urgings of my fellow travelers, I took a thrilling dog sled ride along the side of the mountain and loved every minute!

Helen on the dogsled ride

All too soon, it was time to leave. On the bus to my hotel, I met Ed from Indiana. He and I had been visiting just about the same places. Our paths have crossed often but we have never noticed each other. Ed made me promise to come to the Casino *Kursaal* tonight. I dashed back to the hotel then hurried over to a street market which was about to close for the day. I purchased two cute hand carved wooden cake plates which had Swiss-movement music boxes inside. When you lift the plate up, the music begins; when you place it back on the table, the music ends after the tune is finished playing. It actually alternates between two different melodies!

After much searching, I located a genuine Swiss dinner bell for Mother. The storekeeper was delighted that a foreigner would actually ask for such a bell because they were usually purchased only by the Swiss. The wooden framework was made in China, for which he apologized. He explained that it had to be carved in one piece and Switzerland did not have the right kind of trees for this technique. I had these things shipped to the RMS Queen Mary, and now wonder if I will be able to get them into my cabin on the ship!

After dinner, which tasted scrumptious to a hungry mountain climber, I ambled down to the casino and met Ed. We listened to a lovely orchestra until 10:30, and then went to another place for dancing. Ed told some wild tales of his travels in Russia. When I arrived at the hotel it was locked, but a nice concierge came down in his bathrobe, to let me in.

Date: September 24, 1938
Place: To Montreaux
Weather: Fine but vision not too clear
Timeline: London sets up gas mask distribution centers; France is amassing troops.

This morning, I pulled up stakes at Interlaken and was off for Montreaux.

On the train, I got to talking with the Wendell, an Englishman from Sidney Australia. Wendell plays a great deal of Cricket and travels about reporting on Cricket matches. We discussed everything under the sun while enjoying the lovely Bernese Oberland scenery. It was a marvelous ride along the sides of mountains, dipping down into valleys and up again. As we descended from the top of the final mountain, we saw the whole town of Montreaux laid out before us.

Wendell had no hotel reservation so he tagged along with me to the nearby Terminus Hotel. The clerk assigned him a room right next to mine. It certainly was delightful to have a companion for sightseeing. We had lunch at the hotel and made arrangements for a motorboat ride around the lake and to the Castle of Chillon. As we approached the dock, up came an American girl named Lucille. She worked for NBC in New York City. Lucille turned out to be lots of fun, and the three of us enjoyed Montreaux together.

An entrance to the Castle Chillon

Although one could see a veil over the distant mountains, the sun was shining and the lake was very blue. During our tour of the Castle Chillon we found out that it dates back in part to the eighth century. We saw the various rooms including the chapels, dungeons, and the torture chambers. After our return boat ride, we three relaxed in a tearoom beside the water. My smattering of French has come in handy as I have not encountered any villagers that speak English. After a walk through the town and making a few purchases, we returned to the hotel for dinner.

After dinner, Wendell, Lucille, and I wandered down to the Kursaal Casino. One can find a casino in almost every city in Switzerland. It is a central amusement place. At 8:30 one can listen to an orchestra that plays excellent classical music. Guests sit at little tables and order coffee or drinks. During intermission, people try out their gambling skills. Wendell said he was going to try 5 Francs worth. After losing it all, he sheepishly returned to the concert.

After the concert, there was dancing in the bar room, featuring a Hawaiian orchestra. For being an extremely tall man, Wendell was an excellent dancer. He took many turns around the dance floor, alternating between the two of us. I also danced twice with an extremely good-looking Frenchman, – an excellent dancer – who spoke no English. He seemed to be a part of the place, dancing a lot with the Hawaiian female performer. I felt very flattered when he asked me to dance with him when the orchestra played the last melody before closing time.

When we started home, Wendell demonstrated the exact steps of the Lambeth Walk. We danced and sang all the way. By then, the natives knew beyond a doubt that we were crazy. Here too, we had to rustle the porter out of bed at 1:00 a.m., to let us in. And so, to bed!

Date: September 25, 1938
Place: To Geneva
Weather: Not so good – rain in afternoon.
Timeline: September 25 – 26: The French government decides to commit to defending Czechoslovakia, if the Germans attack. Great Britain indicates that they would stand by France.

Lucille and I had a delightful boat trip from Montreax to Geneva. Upon my arrival, I was met by a representative of the hotel – to my surprise. He was the cutest man, whose eyes were just leaping with laughter. He carried the luggage on a bicycle and I walked over the bridge to my hotel. The room was furnished in a modernistic style; my gracious porter labeled it "*Very American.*"

In the afternoon, we took a sightseeing trip in the rain. We visit numerous monuments and drove out to the place where the yellowish, dirty Arue River joins with the deep blue Rhone. We drove by the Palas des Nations. All nations of the world are represented here, except Germany.

On the way home from dinner, Lucille and I stopped at a sidewalk café to listen to a delightful French orchestra. We tried to drink some beer – nasty stuff!

10

France, and Sailing Home on the RMS Queen Mary

Date: September 26, 1938
Place: Dijon, France
Weather: Rain
Timeline: In a speech in Berlin, Hitler declares that German-speaking citizens in Czechoslovakia are being mistreated. He makes demands for more territories.

There will always be a special place in my heart for Switzerland. The train to Dijon was so absolutely jammed, that I ended up being crowded in a car with seven French people who were talking at the top of their voices. The atmosphere was decidedly tense. Their words flew out so rapidly that my meager knowledge of French failed me. At 12:30 everyone stopped talking and brought out little parcels of paper – from whence appeared their lunches. I too, had my little parcel, so I ate right along with them. After lunch, they resumed their frantic conversations.

It was still raining in mid-afternoon, when the train arrived at Dijon. At the direction of the kind baggage man, I managed to find my way to the Hotel de la Cloche. After walking around in the rain and noting the strange store names: Au Pauvre, Diable, Le Chat Noir, I purchased a silky slip and returned to the hotel. The dining room staff served a marvelous dinner this evening. Dijon is said to be the gastronomic center of France and it truly is. The 1926 Montrachet wine quickly went to my head! By 10 p.m., I could not keep my eyes open any longer.

Date: September 27, 1938
Place: Dijon to Paris
Weather: Mixture – fair in afternoon
Timeline: Hitler now threatens war with Czechoslovakia, to claim the Sudetenland area

It was a comfort to sleep in this morning. After a walk through Dijon, I visited the Museum of Fine Arts, which is touted to be second only to the Louvre. The museum was empty except for a guard in every room. I lingered a little too long with the paintings so had to hurry through the remainder of the museum because it was going to close at Noon.

One guard approached me and warned; “Vous ’avez cinq minutes” “You have five minutes.” When the time was up, I returned to him and said “C’est midi” “It is noon.” He nodded his head and clickety-click he followed me down the staircase and through several galleries that lead to the exit. I was starting to lead a parade! Each room had a guard who was told "C'est midi." He would nod his head, repeat it, and join us. Feeling like the Pied Piper of Hamlin, with all those moustaches marching behind me, I barely resisted the impulse to make a mad dash outside!

Now it was time to return to Paris. The Dijon hotel clerk said that my baggage could be taken to the railway station, but that I would have to find my own transport, since most of the taxi cabs had now been commandeered for the French military service! He said that France was as near to war as it could possibly be - without actually going to battle - and that the troops were partially mobilized.

After wondering how I could possibly get to the railway station, I encountered a sympathetic French porter. He found someone to take me to the train that was headed for Paris.

On the Paris train, I was in a stuffy compartment with a French couple holding a dog who constantly scratched himself. We came upon the remnants of a train crash, which blocked the track for an hour and a half. Since I did not know how long the delay would be, I sat there patiently until the ride resumed.

It really seemed like coming home, to return to the Roune Hotel. Mr. Roffati gave me our old room, too! Everything seems so familiar and comforting. After dinner at the Voltaire Restaurant – with wild strawberries for dessert - I washed my hair, prettied my nails and tumbled into bed.

The Café Voltaire Restaurant

Date: September 28, 1938
Place: Paris France
Weather: OK

This is sailing day! After the familiar hotel breakfast, I finished some last-minute purchases, stopping just long enough for a scanty lunch of rolls and coffee. The train to the RMS Queen Mary dock in Cherbourg was to leave at 3:30, thus I needed to be at the travel office by 2:15.

It was extremely difficult to find a taxi. Paris streets are usually so full of taxicabs that they can hardly move. I found one after twenty minutes, however it took a combination of the hotel manager, the chambermaid, and myself to corner it! The driver told us that not only had most Paris taxis been commandeered for military service, but that two-thirds of the porters at the boat-train station had been mobilized - and it was bedlam! He described how luggage was heaped in huge piles, with no one around to carry it!

As the cab headed for the travel agency, I became more aware of the frantic excitement on the streets. The sides of the buildings served as posting places for huge pieces of paper on which the official news communiqués were written – in longhand. Each of these communiqués had crowds of people standing in front of it.

Upon my arrival at the agency, the travel man said that he expected his son to be called to service at any minute! It was a tense situation, all right. People were trying to leave Paris – trying to get taxis – and trying to get reservations. The French people were preparing for air raids!

I gave up trying to get a porter. Either you transported your own luggage to the train, or it didn't travel with you! I felt sorry for the people struggling with large trunks. By this time, I was toting three suitcases and some packages. The travel agent drove me to the station, and between the two of us, we managed to get my belongings on the boat train to Cherbourg.

When we arrived at the station, we found a madhouse. It seemed like everyone was trying to get out of France. I had met an American girl on the boat train. After our luggage was all stored and our precious sitting places marked, we stood outside and watched the swarms of people streaming down the aisles of the platforms. It looked like all of the remaining taxis in Paris were gathered together there, literally clawing and scratching at each other in an attempt to get close to the station!

When we arrived at Cherbourg it was necessary to board a tender for transportation to the RMS Queen Mary, which was located far out in the harbor instead of at the usual docking place. I heard someone say that she was loaded down with gold that was being shipped from England to the United States, and her standing off was just a precautionary measure. We climbed aboard the tender and waited and waited – literally for hours. The tender just sat there!

It seems that the Queen Mary had been hours late in leaving England (because of the gold, I guess) and she was not ready to receive us. This was the most dreadful afternoon and night! Almost all of the people who were boarding at Cherbourg were from Europe proper. It appeared that most of the people were from the Slavic and Balkan countries, with not very many French or English among them. There we sat, crowded inside this tender, with just masses of people talking in every kind of language. It became very warm in there! Although it was chilly outside and there was no place to sit, we relinquished our precious seats below because we could no longer tolerate the heat and confusion.

We finally reached the Queen Mary at about 10:30 that night, and were herded aboard like cattle. No fooling, I decided this is what steerage must be like. I had not eaten anything since lunch, and there was nothing available to eat until we came on board.

And then - what a disagreeable time! I was acquiring a lovely head cold. Luggage was hopelessly mixed up. We had to relinquish it when we left the boat train and it was put on the Queen Mary for us. The one bag that I wanted – and needed – to get ready for bed, just could not be found. I gave up in despair!

All three of my roommates had previously boarded at Southampton, and were already asleep. I hated to put on the light in our tiny cabin and wake them up. Shivering and sniffling, I climbed to my upper birth and somehow managed to sleep. It was 12:30 a.m!

Date: September 29, 1938
Place: On board the Queen Mary
Weather: Windy and very rough
Timeline: During the Munich Conference, when Hitler promises to make no further demands, France and England agree that he should take possession of the Sudetenland portion of Czechoslovakia.

I finally found my suitcase - under the bunk. Today wasn't much better, as my cold persisted. I had my first taste of seasickness. In an effort to keep out of the way of the others in our cabin, I arose early for breakfast and wandered around a bit, which was difficult to do on an empty stomach. I went to the dining room, but had to leave in the middle of breakfast. In spite of the gale outside, I tried staying on deck for a while. Contrary to all instructions, the longer I remained on the deck (with the sea so rough that standing was almost impossible) the worse I felt. I simply went back to bed. The cabin is very well situated, and if I don't move around I feel fine. Almost everyone on board is seasick.

To my surprise, I received a letter from Arthur, my romantic date at the Café Ostende. I am curious about it but do not feel much like reading right now. I shall wait until tomorrow. And so, to bed.

Date: September 30, 1938
Place: On board Queen Mary
Weather: Fine – still windy
Timeline: The Munich Agreement is signed by Hitler, Chamberlain, Mussolini, and Daladier. Czechoslovakia accepts the agreement and will offer no military resistance. Chamberlain says, "I believe it is peace for our time." Churchill declares the agreement as a total defeat.

What a difference from yesterday, when the boat rocked way up and way down. They shut all the portholes – it was that bad! This morning, although so weak I could barely stand, a sizeable breakfast of figs and oatmeal seemed to be what the doctor ordered. We had to stand in line for 30 minutes, for passport and landing card examination, and to secure a declaration form. Afterward, (still feeling a little squeamish) I obtained an Edgar Wallace detective story from the librarian, betook myself to bed, and got lost in the plot.

Finally recalling the letter from Arthur, I took it out of my bag and proceeded to read:

"My Dear Helen.

I am so sorry that I cannot tell you in English perfectly but I think you understand me in simple words. It is so bad for me that you live far from Budapest. I cannot and will not forget you. All day and night I think always on you. I have so pains in my heart, but I am happy you have a nice journey. You are so lovely and kind to me. How happy I was with you. With much love, ever yours, Arthur."

Date: October 1, 1938
Place: On board the Queen Mary
Weather: Fine
Timeline: German troops occupy the Czechoslovakian Sudetenland.

What happens to a day on shipboard? Poof – it is gone! In the morning I tried to balance my finances to prepare for customs. The boat was beginning to rock again pretty badly, but no one seemed to mind it. I guess a taste of seasickness has cured us all.

My roommates turned out to be very likeable individuals. We spend most of our time inside due to rough weather conditions, but enjoy playing cards and going to the movies. We inspected the other classes and they really are lovely. I feel that the Normandie excels the Queen Mary in many ways, particularly as far as the cuisine is concerned. After dinner, we went to the movie, "The Rage of Paris" with Douglas Fairbanks, Jr. It was extra good. Word was out that there was dancing in the Garden Lounge! I tripped the light fantastic with a big fat man from Seattle. This is the situation - men who like to dance are very scarce on this ship. By my calculations, there is one man for every four women. Competition is fierce! So, the big man from Seattle had fun, dancing up a storm with lots of partners.

Date: October 2, 1938
Place: On board Queen Mary
Weather: Rainy, then fine

This is the last day on board! After breakfast, there was just time to write a short letter before church, which was held in the main lounge of first class. Afterwards, I thoroughly explored first class. I do not think it compares with the Normandie as far as elegance goes, unless I missed seeing some of the important features. Noting the number of people on my Normandie journey, this ship is much more crowded! They say there are 900 people in first class, 800 in tourist, and 600 in third. The indoor swimming pool and children's playrooms were delightful. There is a terrific vibration in tourist class, which would drive one crazy over a long period of time. I returned to my room to do some packing before dinner. All bags had to be ready by 5pm. Luggage now sits in huge piles outside the dining room. We had our last lunch on the Queen Mary today. I was tempted by lentil soup, beet salad, mashed potatoes, roast lamb with mint sauce, and "American apple pie!"

I received a radiogram from Uncle Paul today, and am thrilled that he is going to meet me at the dock. My roommates and I went to tea this afternoon. There, we met a nice fellow who followed us up to the garden lounge, where we listened to music.

Afterward we tried our luck at Keno, which was lots of fun. I actually won! Everyone expected some sort of gala farewell dinner tonight but you would not have known it, except for the menu, which was titled "Auld Lang Syne." Among other items, we were offered grape fruit Manhattan, hot cream of tomato soup, fried parsnips, roast chicken, and ice cream. There was no celebration of any kind. No rip-roaring party, like the one on the Normandie!

Helen on the RMS Queen Mary

Date: October 3, 1938
Place: Home again!
Weather: Fine

This morning the boat was in an uproar with luggage all over the place. We had our last breakfast very early and then, after gathering together hand luggage and coats, we stood in a long, line for passport inspection in First Class. All classes had to go through this. We were arranged in line - American citizens first - and then foreigners. Every once in a while a person would sneak out of the line to peek over the railing to see if someone was on the dock to meet them. I looked for Uncle Paul but had no success. It was too early.

After waiting for what seemed like hours to get our passports examined, we finally disembarked and had the fun of going through customs. I did not mind it at all however they certainly did a very detailed job of examining our things. I guess they must have been expecting some jewel thieves.

My tulip bulbs had to be examined by a special inspector. I had mistakenly reported some of my purchases in terms of German Marks. Judging by the scowls on the inspectors faces, I was in trouble! The officials summoned a special appraisal inspector! He looked at my figures, scared me thoroughly with a nasty scowl, then smiled and walked away without doing a thing. I was finally released from customs and then joyfully discovered that my Uncle Paul was waiting for me! He gathered my luggage and we shoved what seemed like dozens of packages, into a taxi. We sped to the railway station and thence back to Washington DC - where I now spend my days walking around in the clouds.

Chapter 10: France and The RMS Queen Mary

EPILOGUE

Helen continued to correspond with Arthur, the handsome desk man from Budapest. He wrote that he lost his job and was looking for another. She sent him money several times, when he indicated that he had no one else to turn to. He continued to profess his desire to be with her.

Helen resumed foreign travel in the 1960s, after which she enthusiastically explored regions of the world that intrigued her. She visited China soon after it was opened to tourism. She took a cruise down the Amazon River, visited the South Pacific islands, and traveled to Alaska where she rode a bush plane above the Arctic Circle. Her subsequent passports display stamps from Australia, Spain, Singapore, Bangkok, Japan, South Korea, Hong Kong, Kenya, Manila, Tanzania, Zambia, and Egypt, Before each vacation, she would design and sew a mix-and-match wardrobe to wear.

In 1985, my Aunt Helen invited me to join her on a two-week tour of Italy. It was one of the most wonderful two-weeks of my life. I recall that when we landed in Rome, her suitcase did not arrive. I was worried for her, but she seemed confident that her luggage would show up - and it did. Now, that I am familiar with her 1938 trip, and know just how many times she was separated from her luggage, I understand why she refused to worry about it in Italy.

Helen was a kind-hearted and generous person who loved others unconditionally. She is sadly missed

---

Reader please note:

I am including below, two letters from Nazi soldiers that she met on the trip. I have no personal knowledge of their character, or how they conducted themselves during WWII. I am presenting this true story with the photos in a historical fashion, trusting that it will not offend any reader. Please feel free to draw your own conclusions from this book, the photos, and the letters.

Several months after her return, Helen wrote a letter to a friend, which described the trip in great detail. She mentioned that she had received a letter from Hubert, the man who headed a Military Academy in Berlin. Here are her words about his letter:

"I received an interesting letter from Hubert last November, which I must say I have not answered. He wrote that he had been in on the military conferences concerning the annexation of the Sudetenland and was with the first German troops, which marched into Czechoslovakia. I was rather interested in his description of the joy and shouts of welcome, which greeted the Germans. It was very vivid and rather contrary to the general opinion that we have, in America. Of course, he is a Nazi and it couldn't be anything else to him."

At the end of her letter to the friend, Helen added:

"You see, this was just the time before the Munich Peace Pact was signed and I guess the countries were about as near war as they could be While in Germany, I had seen many soldiers, but there did not seem to be a great feeling of anxiousness. I believe now that things were bad there, and we didn't realize it over here. From all I have read since then and from the facts related by my parents, when I returned, I now know just how serious the situation was."

Here is the content of Hubert's Letter which was written in broken English, in November of 1938:
November 16, 1938
"Dear Helen:
I have much enjoyed your letter, many thanks indeed. I had not hoped to hear anything from you after our farewell in Vienna.

Many thanks also, for your snapshots, you have sent. Was it not a jolly occasion our riding on the Vienna Express.... I often and willingly make remembrance of the hours in the Rathouse Cellar, the Grinzing wine and Hungarian music.

I am glad to hear that you enjoyed your stay in our country. I hope you found many interesting and meaningful things, and that you found a friendly and hospitable population. The Germans are not so bad animals as they perhaps are described in your newspapers.

Meantime I have had many interesting and important works. You must surely have heard of the Czechoslovakian Crisis, the political tension, the Munich Conference and its military consequences. With all those events, I was in high military staff meetings, and you can understand that it was very interesting for me.

I was in the first groups that entered into Czechoslovakia. It was an overwhelming impression I never could forget. It is impossible to describe the enthusiasm of the population. Every soldier was considered as a deliverer. You scarcely can fancy the oppression and the harm that the population had suffered under the old regime, and joy finally, after several hundred years' struggle, to have returned home.

I never before had seen so much movement of souls and so many tears of joy as in Sudetenland. The year 1938 will always remain a year of joy and pride for all Germans. It is the year in which the German people hitherto, spread over the three European countries, and had found its definitive form in one Reich. I hope you willingly will remember all your impressions in Germany. Beg your pardon for all the mistakes I have made in this letter. The results of my English lessons at school are not important. Thank you again for your letter and the pleasant times at Vienna.
Sincerely Yours, Hubert"

Helen brought home a newsletter from the Queen Mary. The date is September 30, 1938.

The headline reads *"Early Results of the Munich Conference."*

The main article headline was *"Token Occupation of Outer Sudetenland areas by German Troops."*

Another article was topped by the headline: *"Deliverance from Calamity"* with the subtitle: *"Hopes for removal of Czech Fears and German Grievances."*

I will let you, dear reader, draw your own conclusions.

After the war was over, Helen received a letter from Max, the Austrian soldier in Nuremberg. It is typewritten in German. I was fortunate to find someone who could expertly translate it. This is what it said:

August 18, 1945

"Dear respected, Beloved Helen,

Six years have gone by that I have been without a sign of life from you. Your Christmas wishes in 1939 reached my hands, but I do not know if you received my answer to them. In this time frame, there has been a lot of change here and probably in your fatherland as well. What all happened I cannot tell you in details, it would be a letter of suffering. I want to bring you joy with my lines.

I hope you can still remember me at all, your European boyfriend? I thought of you often and would have been happy to have exchanged thoughts and ideas with you through this hard time. To refresh your memory, I have enclosed a picture that you sent to me at one time (train station Nuremberg.) Due to bombing damages, I moved with my family to Bad Ischl in a country house. My apartment in Linz is being restored. The rebuilding work has thank God started. There is a large deficit of workers and materials, and especially food. The need is large!

We are living in the area of your people's occupied zone and we have already started relations with them, as we had to clear out our country house within a few hours after they arrived to make room for their quarters. A few days later, we were allowed to move back in after these troops were pulled out. In November we will be in Linz again. I manage the business from Bad-Ishl until my apartment in Linz is ready to move back into. The connection to your people here has not yet bettered my English to the extent to write in English. Maybe one day. Did your German get better? If yes, then you are perfect, since you already could write understandable German.

It will interest you that in the meantime, I married and have a family of four daughters and my dear wife, with whom I have a happy marriage. The biggest worry that we have at the time, is to feed these always hungry four mouths. Almost all of the goods have been destroyed or stolen throughout the war and its aftermath. We all thank God that this cruel fighting of mankind has found an end.

You should be congratulated to be a citizen of the biggest nation in the world. We are again separated from Germany and are trying to become an independent and free land. Since our economy is almost on ground bottom, we really need help from stronger nations, especially America. We will not let our courage sink and will use all of our energy to make our Austria, that is unfortunately mostly confused with Germany, into a country where everyone is free and can feel comfortable. In a few years, we hope that we are so far to secure a comfortable stay for the many foreigners that will visit us.

Now, dear Helen, how has it been with you? Maybe this letter will not reach you because in the meantime, you maybe also got married and carry another name? I am exceptionally interested what changes have happened to my American girlfriend. Let's hope that this letter has reached your hands, and you can write to me, too.

This letter was sent through a US citizen who lives in Linz as a soldier for the American occupation. He will forward this with his mail to the USA and his wife will forward it to you. Maybe it is possible to get an answer from you through the same way? I will ask the man that mediated to give you his US address so that you can write to him. He will then forward to me. You, my dear Helen, are heartfully greeted by my wife, my family and especially from me, who wishes you all the best. May there be a good fate that might happen, that you are once again able to come to Europe to visit our beautiful, but at the moment poor country. I have made plans to come to the USA to buy machines for a spinnery weaving mill and ropes/cables for my father-in-law. I do not want to miss this chance to pay my respects to you. Again, my deepest greetings and wishes, Your European friend from Ober-Oesterreich (Austria)
P.S. – Could you send me brochures for ropes/cables and spinning machines for hemp?"

End of Epilogue

Additional Photos:

One last photo of Helen and her friend, Margy, on the SS Normandie –

Salzburg, taken from the fortress area

Approaching Castle Chillon by water

www.ingramcontent.com/pod-product-compliance
Lightning Source LLC
Chambersburg PA
CBHW070631030426
42337CB00020B/3977
9780983819608